CONVERSATIONS WITH KIAROSTAMI

CONVERSATIONS WITH KIAROSTAMI

BY GODFREY CHESHIRE

**foreword by
AHMAD KIAROSTAMI**

**edited by
JIM COLVILL**

**translations by
TANIA AHMADI**

Woodville Press · New York

in collaboration with
**KIAROSTAMI
FOUNDATION**

ISBN: 978-0-9994683-5-7
Library of Congress Control Number: 2019945593

Published by Woodville Press, New York.
woodvillepress@gmail.com

Fifth Printing (2024)
Printed in Spencer, Indiana by World Arts.

Foreword © 2019 Ahmad Kiarostami.
All other text © 2019 Godfrey Cheshire.
Film stills from *Close-Up* appear courtesy of Celluloid Dreams.
All other film stills appear courtesy of mk2.

Front cover: detail of a still from Kiarostami's *Homework*.

For Ahmad and Bahman

CONTENTS

Foreword by Ahmad Kiarostami 9
Introduction 13

Conversations with Kiarostami 23
    "Bread and Alley" 26
    "Breaktime" 34
    Experience 39
    The Traveler 42
    "So Can I" 50
    "Two Solutions for One Problem" 53
    A Wedding Suit 56
    "The Colors" 62
    "Tribute to the Teachers" 64
    The Report 67
    "Solution" 84
    "Jahan Nama Palace" 86
    Case No. 1, Case No. 2 89
    "Toothache" 94
    "Orderly or Disorderly" 97
    "The Chorus" 99
    Fellow Citizen 102
    First Graders 107
    Where Is the Friend's House? 109
    Close-Up 130
    And Life Goes On 139
    Through the Olive Trees 153
    Taste of Cherry 161
    The Wind Will Carry Us 170

Appendix:
    The Iranian Who Won The World's Attention 179

Thanks / Author bio

FOREWORD

IN 2005 OR 2006, THERE WAS a screening of *Close-Up* at the San Francisco Museum of Modern Art, and Godfrey Cheshire was the guest speaker. I had recently moved to San Francisco and was very excited to see my friend Godfrey there. In his presentation, he said how everyone in the film is getting "bamboozled": the Ahankhah family by Hossein Sabzian, the cab driver by the reporter, Sabzian by cinema, and everyone, including the audience, by Kiarostami. As an example, he said how most of the court scene is not real and is just a setup by Kiarostami. After the event, I told Godfrey how I enjoyed the talk, but also that what he said about the court scene not being real was wrong. I remembered my father taking the camera to the court and filming the scene. I had also seen him talking about it, both while he was editing the film and after screenings. I was sure. Also, visually it was clear: while the film was shot in 35mm, the court scene was shot in 16mm and this was because they couldn't take a 35mm camera to the court. Godfrey responded by telling me I was wrong and that most of the court scene was shot afterward—that all those conversations with the "second camera" didn't happen in the court. I knew Godfrey was wrong and offered to contact my father and ask him about this. It was a late night in San Francisco, and morning in Tehran, so it was a good time to call. I called my father, told him the story, and asked which one of us was right. There was a long pause on the other side of the line, and then he said: "Godfrey is right."

During Godfrey's several visits to Iran throughout a decade, he formed a relationship with my father that I had rarely seen him having with other writers. I believe this was because of Godfrey's ability to go beyond the surface; his unique views and interpretations. While Godfrey considers the environment of the stories, he manages to stay away from cliché and looks for personal fingerprints that make common stories special, which is exactly what my father did with his films. It is well-known that Godfrey was one of the first people who introduced the Iranian cinema to America and, yet, there is no trace of the usual "exotic" approach in Godfrey's view of it. That is what you will find in this book: a refreshing conversation with Abbas that has substance, and is far from cliché.

Abbas spent the first half of his filmmaking career making films for or about children at Kanoon, the Center for the Intellectual Development for Children and Young Adults. Then, with *Close-Up*, he moved on to films about adults. One of his later films at Kanoon, *Where Is the Friend's House?*, brought him international recognition. While his post-*Where Is the Friend's House?* cinema is well-known, his earlier films have not been seen much outside of Iran and, as a result, haven't received much discussion. In his interviews, Godfrey talks to Abbas about these early films and provides a unique opportunity to learn more about what my father thought about cinema, art, and life in general, from these early days.

Abbas often said that he only made half the film, that the other half was made in the audience's mind. This is how he saw poetic cinema, which was his cinema. Godfrey is able to create a beautiful second half, and reading his take on my father's films always provides a more beautiful and complete image, something you can see in these interviews. What makes this book even better is that, beyond his beautiful interpretations of the films, Godfrey also makes sure to get the facts right. This gives the readers a much more complete image, and a unique window into the mind of my father, an image that I completely trust because, by now, I know "Godfrey is right."

    Ahmad Kiarostami
    2019

INTRODUCTION

Abbas Kiarostami was always generous with me in conversation. Whether answering my questions in an interview situation, or just chatting at his home in Tehran or in the many other places where we saw each other over more than 20 years of friendship, he always responded with genial engagement. In the early years of our knowing each other, his English was minimal, my Farsi practically non-existent. But, whether or not a translator was used, he found a way to connect with my comments and convey his own.

I initially encountered his work in 1992 at the first festival of post-Revolutionary Iranian films held in New York, at Lincoln Center. My first exposure to any Iranian cinema, this festival, which I was enlisted to cover for *Film Comment*, offered an eye-opening trove of films by masters such as Dariush Mehrjui and Bahram Beyzai. I didn't know at the time that in Iran these and other directors were ranked higher than Kiarostami. I only knew that his *Close-Up* struck me as one of the most extraordinary films I'd ever seen. In the article I wrote about the festival, I gave pride of place to that film and two other Kiarostami features, *Where Is the Friend's House?* and *And Life Goes On*.

That first encounter with Iranian cinema led to an ongoing fascination that became a critical specialization. In the years that followed, Kiarostami quickly emerged as the most acclaimed Iranian filmmaker on the world stage. I first met him in 1994, when *Through the Olive Trees*—which joined *Where Is the Friend's House?* and *And Life Goes On* in what critics would call the Koker Trilogy—played the New York Film Festival. Seeking to understand the film culture he emerged from, I asked him about his earliest memories of movies.

He replied: "At the time films with heroes like Ulysses and Hercules were popular but I liked Italian films that showed young people riding through the streets on motorcycles. What I really cared about were beautiful men and women. The first time I saw a movie that shocked me was *La Dolce Vita*. And for the first time I tried to find out who made the movie. That was the first film that made me fascinated with moviemaking. The second was *La Strada*."

The Italian connection made sense, even if the conditions of the Islamic Republic didn't allow for lissome girls and boys flitting around Tehran on Vespas; critics had already noted the kinship with some post-Revolutionary films and the work of Italy's neorealists. But the thing I was most curious about, I told Kiarostami, was the sense conveyed by these new films that Iran could seemingly be both medieval and post-modern at once (what happened to the connecting tissue of modernism?), and the question of whether the complex self-reflexivity of *Close-Up* reflected a remarkable Iranian sophistication of filmgoers, or just of certain filmmakers.

"I think it's a universal situation: There are good audiences and bad audiences everywhere," he responded. "In Iran, there are sophisticated audiences and illiterate audiences. Here I've found there are some unsophisticated audiences. The woman who complains [in the New York Film Festival public screening] that the ending of *Through the Olive Trees* isn't clear... this isn't my kind of audience. Many audiences go to movies to satisfy some basic emotion; they don't necessarily like my films."

My curiosity about the cinematic conditions in Iran, for filmmakers as well as filmgoers and critics, began to get more answers when I started visiting there in 1997. I found that cinema had become an industry and an art form of unusual importance in the Islamic Republic, for several reasons. While the country had built a fairly robust commercial cinema characterized by non-exportable mediocre comedies and action films including numerous, partly propagandistic movies about the Iran-Iraq War, the much smaller art-film sector had been cultivated and supported by moderate and liberal elements in the government, who saw it as a way of winning friends and influencing opinion internationally, as well as building on Iran's age-old reputation for artistic sophistication and originality.

But not all of the government's cultural functionaries were in agreement. Kiarostami began his career running the filmmaking division of the Center for the Intellectual Development of Children and Young Adults (a government organization that Iranians call Kanoon), which produced all but a few of his films through *And Life Goes On* in 1992. At that time, an incursion of hardliners into the culture ministry resulted in his losing his post at Kanoon. While international support and his own resources allowed him to go on making films, Kiarostami's position within the Iranian cultural hierarchy grew less and less comfortable.

When I visited him at his home in Tehran for the first time, in February of 1997, he was clearly in a period of stress. Since *And Life Goes On* and *Through the Olive Trees* had gained considerable acclaim at the Cannes Film Festival, expectations were high for the film he was supposed to deliver in 1997. But Kiarostami, then and in the weeks after, seemed beleaguered on several fronts. His non-admirers in the bureaucracy gave him the least-congenial editing slots. Some of the new film had been ruined in the lab and would have to be reshot. And there were already official frowns provoked by word that the film concerned suicide, a taboo under Islam.

The weeks leading up to *Taste of Cherry*'s scheduled screening at Cannes were a time of nerve-wracking high drama. The word from Iran was that the government wouldn't permit the film to leave the country. This news generated some critical international news coverage (including a front-page article in *Variety* that I contributed to) which Kiarostami's supporters were able to use to suggest that the incident was damaging Iran's reputation globally. Discussions about the film's fate reportedly went to the top of the Iranian government, yet when I left New York for Cannes two days before the festival began, it was still unclear if it would make it to France.

That the film made it to Paris in time to be subtitled and then to Cannes for its screening seemed well-nigh miraculous. But these events only paved the way for the real miracle: its win of the Palme d'Or (shared with Shohei Imamura's *The Eel*). As I've written in other places, the impression that the film was greeted with universal praise simply wasn't true. *Taste of Cherry* and later Kiarostami films divided critics, though in a way that made for some of the decade's most interesting critical discussions.

The film and its win of the Palme d'Or did, in any case, establish Kiarostami at the front ranks of world auteurs, a reality that was evident even that evening. After he accepted the award (along with a brief kiss from Catherine Deneuve, which ignited a firestorm of criticism back home) and attended the obligatory press conference, he and I had a drink near the ocean. He seemed more bemused than elated. When we walked along the Croisette to the festival dinner, few people recognized him until we approached the assembled paparazzi, whose flashes soon engulfed him in a cone of strobing lights—and perhaps gave him his own *La Dolce Vita* moment.

After Cannes, Kiarostami returned to Tehran and the fundamentalists' protest over Deneuve's kiss. I followed him a few weeks later, in time to attend his 57th birthday party in a friend's villa outside the city, and stayed to interview filmmakers during the remainder of the summer. Most of the interviews in this book belong to this period and were done over a few days in August. As I did with other directors, I asked Kiarostami to discuss his career with me film by film. We began talking in his basement office in his house. After some time, when it became apparent that our rate of progress wouldn't be sufficient to finish the discussion before he had to leave for the Locarno Film Festival, he proposed that he drive me up to see the remains of Koker and we continue the interview as we went.

Roughly speaking, the portion of the interview material here concerning the Koker Trilogy, *Taste of Cherry* and *Close-Up* were done on this trip, when we were accompanied by translator Parto Mohtadi and Kiarostami's son Bahman, then 19. Needless to say, it was both fascinating and moving to discuss the Koker films while visiting the locale itself. The place had been a living village during the making of *Where Is the Friend's House?* Abandoned after the earthquake of 1990, and revived only briefly to play roles in *And Life Goes On* and *Through the Olive Trees*, it looked like it had been empty and ravaged by the elements for hundreds of years, not less than a decade. Only the hill with the zig-zag path, created to Kiarostami's specifications, seemed largely unchanged.

We also encountered some of the films' human elements. As we drove up to Koker, Kiarostami was hailed by a young man who'd had small parts in some of them. And reaching the town of Rostamabad, we ran across Hossein Rezai, the tea boy who becomes a bit player in *And Life Goes On* and then the star of that film's sequel.

In retrospect, these interviews have an interesting correlation with the path of Kiarsotami's work. Looking back on his oeuvre following his death in 2016, I began to view his career as dividing into three periods, each roughly 15 years in length. The first, which I call the Kanoon period, stretches from his 1970 inaugural short, "Bread and Alley," through the documentary feature *First Graders* in 1984. The second period, which I call the Masterworks period (though it contains his three final Kanoon productions), encompasses the 1989 documentary feature *Homework* along with the six films that made him a celebrated figure worldwide in the '90s, from the Koker Trilogy and *Close-Up* through *Taste of Cherry* to *The Wind Will Carry Us* in 1999. Beginning with the documentary *ABC Africa* in 2001, what I call his Experimental period marked his turn to low-budget digital filmmaking and sporadic work abroad; it includes films such as *Ten*, *Certified Copy* and *Like Someone in Love* and culminates with the computer animated *24 Frames* (completed by his son Ahmad and posthumously released in 2017).

The interviews assembled here (including one conducted after the premiere of *The Wind Will Carry Us* in Venice in 1999) cover the first two periods of his work as defined above. As such, they allow us to observe his career's early evolution and the way he viewed his work after having attained the peak represented by the Palme d'Or. In essence, the main differences between the first and second periods concerned the conditions under which he worked and the attention his work received. In the first period, working mostly in the relatively artisan-like anonymity of Kanoon, he was free to experiment and develop his own style, and his films usually reached only small audiences, even in Iran. From the time when *Where Is the Friend's House?* took several prizes at the 1989 Locarno Film Festival, however, he concentrated on making dramatic features which reached important, interested audiences of cinephiles and critics outside of Iran. Yet something about the world's spotlight ultimately seemed not to agree with him, so it was perhaps natural that he retreated to a more experimental stance with a degree of Kanoon-like creative freedom in his eclectic final period.

These interviews also mark a certain stage in my efforts to understand Kiarostami's films and their cultural contexts, both cinematic and Persian. Though I had been writing about his work for five years, in 1997 I was still very early in a process that would continue in future years, and continues still. While in Iran that summer, I not only interviewed numerous filmmakers and cultural figures, I immersed myself in learning about the Iranian cinema's "New Wave" of the late '60s and '70s and revival in the '80s, and also reading about Iranian history, art and literature, both ancient and modern. These investigations helped me construct an intellectual framework for approaching Kiarostami's work, yet, as I say, this effort was still at an early stage when the interviews were conducted. I didn't, for example, delve much into the influence of poetry on Kiarostami's cinematic methods until pondering *The Wind Will Carry Us*. And my thoughts on the autobiographical dimension of his films, while informed by his comments on *The Traveler* and *The Report*, would continue to grow in future years as I got to know him better.

Although some of the material here was used in a profile of Kiarostami I wrote for the *New York Times* in September, 1997 (see Appendix), the interviews were not conducted with the intent of being published. They are being brought out now to coincide with the release of restorations of many Kiarostami films, a project jointly executed by France's mk2 and the Criterion Collection in the US; the films will be included in a touring retrospective of the director's work. These restorations and the releases are particularly exciting because they include the films of Kiarostami's Kanoon period, most of which have never been released and only rarely seen previously.

These early films are fascinating both in themselves and how they relate to his later work. And they indicate the diversity of his means and motives while working at Kanoon. In interviews, he often said the films were "about, but not necessarily for, children"—an apt description of his first four films ("Bread and Alley," "Breaktime," *Experience* and *The Traveler*), a remarkable group of moody, mercurial little black-and-white art films. But immediately thereafter, in "So Can I," "Two Solutions for One Problem" and "The Colors," he made films that obviously were primarily for young audiences. The interest in children continued and also encompassed the concern with early education in the Islamic Republic evident in his two feature-length documentaries *First Graders* and *Homework*. In addition to children-as-subjects, there are notable depictions of adolescent sensibilities and conflicts in *Experience* and *A Wedding Suit*, the latter a gem-like masterpiece that anticipates the accomplishments of *Where Is the Friend's House?* This rich period also includes the bold inventiveness of the extraordinary *Case No. 1, Case No. 2* and the droll *Fellow Citizen*, idiosyncratic experiments with sharp satiric undertows.

I hope these interviews will help orient viewers in their encounters with the newly available films of the Kanoon period as well as the restored masterworks. The first critical study I wrote about Kiarostami, for *Film Comment*, was headlined "A Cinema of Questions." That characterization was all but inevitable given how much time characters in his films spend asking questions, or being asked them. Beyond that, the films themselves seem to pose endless series of questions. Two

Solutions? Orderly or disorderly? Life or death? I was lucky in being able to ask the man himself questions of my own, and he was kind enough to give me detailed, thoughtful answers. I trust his generosity to me will also benefit the readers of this book.

Godfrey Cheshire
New York, June 2019

CONVERSATIONS WITH KIAROSTAMI

Cheshire: *Can you tell me about your education?*

Kiarostami: I went to university to study painting in 1959 and spent thirteen years there. Although the duration was supposed to be only four years, I stayed for thirteen years. In those days I held the record for those thirteen years. The reason it took me so long is that I was working. That was the only reason. I did graphic work for advertisements, and was making commercials. I also made opening titles for films.

And you got into filmmaking through illustrating children's books?

Yes, I illustrated three children's books. Then, with my experience in advertisements, I founded Kanoon's center for filmmaking. [Kanoon: the Center for the Intellectual Development for Children and Young Adults, a government organization.]

You founded the center for filmmaking, but Kanoon had existed previously, right?

Yes. Kanoon already existed as a publishing house.

What government ministry was it under?

It was set up by Farah, the wife of the Shah. My film "Bread and Alley" was the first film produced at this center.

How did you happen to found the center for filmmaking?

I'd made an advertisement that people thought was made in a foreign country, as its quality was very good. It was a commercial about a heater. And, I'd made four commercials about banks in which children acted. All these commercials were very successful. Because of this I was asked to make films for children by Firooz Shirvanlou, head of the Department of Culture at Kanoon.

Did he ask you to set up the filmmaking center at the same time?

When I started we set up the center first, and then I made films. I was already familiar with Kanoon through making my commercials.

And you worked there until fairly recently?

Yes. Up until six years ago, when radical elements came to Kanoon.

So for over 20 years?

Yes.

Did you have a title during that time?

First I was the head of the Cinema Department, and then I had the title of Director.

I take it you oversaw the production of all films made there, not just yours?

Just for a couple of years. After that, no. I became the head of a department at Kanoon that produced educational films for children. I understood better than anyone else that my films were not films *for* children. They were films *about* children, not children's films.

While you were making films, you were also working as an administrator or producer at Kanoon?

Yes, for a while. Especially for the educational films.

Did you always want to make films, or was this something you discovered once you had the opportunity at Kanoon?

I think it was fate. My mind was always curious about the problems human beings face, ever since my childhood. Initially, I didn't explore this curiosity through film—that happened along the way.

I never considered myself a cinephile. I still don't. Perhaps this is because I cannot easily find films I like. Maybe every two or three years I find a film that moves me, which leads me to believe that I'm also a cinephile.

I've a theory that there are two types of filmmakers. One kind, if you took away the cinema, they would turn to some other medium, like painting or music or writing. The other kind, if you took away cinema, they wouldn't know what to do. They're only about cinema.

I'm the first kind. Sometimes, I wouldn't mind if they took cinema away from me. I wouldn't say I wish they would, just that I wouldn't mind if they did.

"Bread and Alley"
(12 mins., B&W, 1970)

"The mother of all my films," according to Kiarostami, starts out as a breezily observed anecdote about a boy wending his way home through Tehran alleys carrying a loaf of bread. Both the boy, and the old man he sees and begins to follow, will factor into future Kiarostami films, as will the use of "dead time," the journey structure, and the poetic articulation of space. The final scene, involving a dog and a door, ends on a note of wry ambiguity.

Cheshire: *Let's talk about "Bread and Alley." It's the first and, I think, one of the best of your short films. What do you remember about making it?*

Kiarostami: I saw it recently with an audience and felt that I've carried all the faults of this first film with me up until now. Similarly, if "Bread and Alley" has some good points, you can also find them in my other films. This reminds me of something Mr. [Akira] Kurosawa said that was very strange. His assistant screened *The Traveler* for him and, after the film was over, he told his assistant that Kiarostami hadn't changed at all. He said that he didn't know whether this was a compliment to me or not. I replied that I didn't know either. There are things about "Bread and Alley" that are repeated in my other films; it's the mother of my other films.

I had problems with my cameraman when I was making the film. I still have difficulties with cinematographers, but now at least they'll listen to me. But, for this film, the cameraman wouldn't listen to me. Now I'd like to find him and say: after 28 years, let's sit down and watch the film and see which one of us

didn't do his job. [*Laughs*] His camera was shaking a lot. He also interfered in the editing process. There was a shot I wanted all in one piece—it's the last shot, when the child and the dog come and stop at the door. The child rings the bell and goes inside, and the dog tries to go in as well. But, the person who opened the door closes it on the dog. The dog lies down and puts its head on its paws, and then when another child comes to the alley, the dog lifts its head and looks at that child. This was all in my script and I had written it as one shot. But the cameraman said that we had to shoot the scene piece by piece. I said, no, it all must happen in one shot. And it was obvious that the dog wasn't professional, the kid wasn't professional—and I was an amateur as well! All three of us created big problems for the cameraman. He was always angry. And to get this shot, the last shot, we were shooting for 30 days. It took one month for this one scene to be fully shot.

You tried filming it every day for 30 days?

We kept repeating it but it didn't work. Every day. I wanted the scene to happen at around noon. Therefore we had half an hour to get this shot, because the shadows would change, and we couldn't film anymore. We were really working as non-professionals. Sometimes the dog wouldn't do it right, or the kid wouldn't perform correctly. But, finally, the whole thing happened in one shot. Everything happened the way I wanted it to. And, even then, I wasn't fully satisfied—I said that we had to do it again for the film negative! That's when the cameraman took out his light meter, put it down, and said that he was quitting. He said that I was crazy and that what happened a few minutes earlier had been a mere coincidence. And he was right. But I was also right, because I'd frequently tell him that I liked the kind of shots that would happen accidentally, not the ones we'd set. Once it was done, to me the shot looked dead. Therefore, "Bread and Alley" was a very good experience.

I find your use of "dead time" interesting. Like when the kid is just standing there and scratching his head.

I think that in shots where nothing is happening there's only the appearance of nothing happening. There's always internal development. You have to create an atmosphere where the expectation of the audience is the same as the expectation of the character. At a certain point, character and audience must become one.

I've written about your way of "decentering" narrative. Your stories often don't start at the expected place. Nor do they end at the expected place.

We can only watch life in a film from a certain point, and then must leave it at a certain point. We have to interrupt it and stop. But life doesn't end there. You have to decide on the ending point yourself; but this end isn't the end of the film, it's just the end of our time watching the film.

One thing I notice about your films involving children is that you take them seriously. You look at them from a child's point of view. I think many directors, perhaps unconsciously, literally look down on children. Also, it seems that you have a real fascination with space. In this film specifically, it's the world of alleys that the story takes place in. Your camera doesn't separate character from space—the character and the space are always seen together.

In my opinion, the location is one of the most important parts of a film. It's where all the events find their purpose, something like a costume for an actor. My characters have no meaning if separated from their location. You cannot erase the background behind me, can you? When at the location, usually those who pass by are the types of people that I want. This is why I always try to find my actors on location, in the neighborhoods where my films take place, and nowhere else. Location comes first. It gives me ideas. If I ever see that the location doesn't match my concept, then I'll change my concept. The location is more important. This is my paradigm.

Did you have an ability to direct children from this first film, or did you develop that? And do you choose children based on how they look or their ability to act?

I'm lucky to have never been on the set of anyone else's film, or been anyone else's assistant. I've also never studied filmmaking.

I think these things contribute to my ability to direct children. When I talk to film students, I see how conservatively they view things and how close-minded they are. I used to say it's better to learn all the theories and rules of filmmaking so you can then throw them out the window. But then I realized that it's difficult to forget when you have spent so much time learning. When my son Bahman wanted to study filmmaking I proposed he forget the idea, and eventually he studied graphics instead. I believe that, in this way, he learned what he was really meant to do.

I want to quote an Italian director, Ermanno Olmi. He beautifully said something like: "The first generation of cinema looked at life and made films. The second generation looked at life, and the films of the first generation, and made films based on that. The third and fourth generations looked at the films of the previous generations and made films from them." I think it has been forgotten that films are supposed to depict life. The first generation of filmmakers that I respect so much never attended film schools—none of the great film directors studied filmmaking. The experiences we acquire in life are more important. It seems that sometimes filmmakers feel that just because new equipment is available, it's their duty to use it. I've witnessed many of my colleagues strive to take a certain shot for their film but, for whatever reason, the conditions aren't favorable: they don't have the necessary equipment, the weather conditions aren't good, or there isn't enough money. They hold onto the idea and use the shot for their next film, even though sometimes it shouldn't have anything to do with the next film.

Each film has its own possibilities. For example, I cannot work with a given child in the same way I worked with another child in a previous film—each child is different. Not only children: all individuals. You cannot make films based on general rules. This includes both the technical and the emotional aspects. With some people you cannot bring the camera too close to them, because they feel it to be too overbearing. With them you have to consider the distance, so you must change your lens. Therefore, the spirit of the actor ultimately indicates which lens you should use. In a sense, even they direct the film. Actors specify where to cut, because their strength designates how long my shot can last.

One of the problems that my cameramen have with me is that they think I spoil my actors. I do spoil them, because they're the ones who say the final words. I must adjust according to their state of mind. Their state of mind is the most important thing as it transfers meaning to the audience. This is the most important rule to learn. All other cinematographic rules can change under the influence of this one.

It seems there must be a balance between letting a child actor simply go, in order to be natural, and controlling them for the sake of time.

Exactly. I think this is where experience helps. There's a Persian poem by Rumi that's very beautiful, and feels like it is recommending how to work with actors. It goes:

> You are my ball, and you roll because
> of the strike of my polo mallet.
> Just remember,
> it is me who is chasing you
> even though it is me who is helping you run.

I both make you run, and I run after you. This rule seems to me very right. The actor is independent from me, but, in the end, it's I who have to put the actor in motion. It takes time, expertise, and experience. And I must understand this rule of the game:

that the ball doesn't always go where I want it to go. I can only correct it. Rumi's poem applies this to something that doesn't have a soul and is just an inanimate object, but I must consider a human being which is much more complicated than that.

Someone once asked me why I work with non-professionals, and I replied that it's because they don't listen to me. By not listening to me they show that they're alive. They never say that they can't do it but, if they don't want to do something, I can see it in their eyes. That's when I need to change things so that I do see them wanting to do it. When the actor acts well in the first take, it means this role belongs to them and that I didn't make a wrong decision. But when they can't act, it means that I have made a mistake. When the actor can't do it three times in a row, it means that they won't be able to do it for the rest of the day, and I need to leave them alone. I must give this person a rest, let time pass, and come back tomorrow—then they can correct. The most important thing about non-professional actors is that, in reality, they're the director and also the writer. They're illiterate, they don't know cinema, but without knowing it they're still creating the film. This kind of cinema is, to me, director/actor cinema, meaning that it's the combined work of the two. Both have to work hard to establish a mutual understanding.

You put a big emphasis on choosing the actor in the first place, so that you're assured of having the right person to work with.

Exactly. I've an image in my mind and so have to search to find the closest person to this image. But, when I find him, he'll not be one hundred percent similar to my idea. Therefore, the key to my success is that I don't try to change that part of him. I must change myself according to his potential. In the end this doesn't have to do with filmmaking, it's about the relationship between two people. You should only have control over yourself; other people aren't under your control. If I'm trying to have a good relationship with an actor it's better for me to change than to expect the other person to change—I've more power over myself than over others.

"Breaktime"
(14 mins., B&W, 1972)

Disciplined at school for breaking a window, a boy joins throngs of his schoolmates as they make a cacophonous exit into Tehran's streets. He then briefly joins an impromptu soccer game but disrupts it by stealing the ball and running away, ultimately drifting aimlessly along a busy highway. Dialogue-less but using non-synchronous concrete sound throughout, the moody film shows Kiarostami expanding his visual vocabulary with zooms, crane and helicopter shots.

Cheshire: *Let's talk about "Breaktime." One thing I notice about that it is that you use some very complicated shots, like a crane shot combined with a zoom, and you never use shots like this afterwards.*

Kiarostami: This is a great point. It's related to the same issue I mentioned before. In some films you can't do certain things and so save them for your next film. This was my mistake. However, it wasn't just my mistake. It was also the mistake of the critics. After "Bread and Alley" was released, people loved that film very much. Foreign critics loved it. We also received first prize at the Tehran Children's Film Festival. However, Iranian critics asserted that I didn't know the alphabet of cinema, and they were right. So for this, my second film, there was a lot of pressure on me. I thought I had to take advantage of all the possibilities of cinema, as the critics wanted me to. When the film was finished I was so ashamed of it. In the end, a lot of it was thrown in the garbage. It had tracking shots, zooms, and so on. For example, there was this very bad tracking shot, when the kid was walking along a wall, that could've been shot with

a simple pan. I'd taken all manner of film equipment with me to the set, and because I hadn't yet used this traveling device I thought I should use it then. I didn't need all that equipment. You might not believe it, but I even took helicopter shots and then threw them out. I wanted to somehow convince the critics and prove to them that I was able to take helishots, tracking shots, zoom-ins, and so on.

I do really like the idea of the film, because it doesn't tell a story. My ideal cinema is a cinema that doesn't narrate a story, but instead wants to explore a subject. Of course, each film tells a story anyway, but cinema has a more important role than just this.

This is what interests me about "Breaktime." That it doesn't tell a story. What happens in it sets up an analogy for your work. When it opens, the little boy is standing in a hall because he's being punished. But then he runs away, and that's like you running away from the story.

That's right. In my view, there's an atmosphere that persists throughout the film, and it's an atmosphere of anxiety. If you asked me to explain the film in one word, that one word would be "anxiety." This anxiety, in the instances where there are closed spaces and closed frames, derives from those rules that have been set for mankind. In my view the boy's anxiety isn't much different from that of Hossein Sabzian [protagonist of *Close-Up*]. When he gets out of school, this doesn't change: the space opens up but the feelings within him don't change. In my view, this is what is important.

I visited Czechoslovakia many times during the Communist regime, since I had a lot of close friends there. I went there more recently and saw big stores: there was a McDonald's, and many tourists walking around in colorful clothes. But nothing had truly changed. They had become part of the "free world," but they still closed their stores at five o'clock. At six o'clock the town was dead. Something very deep must happen in order to truly change a human being. So, in "Breaktime," the boy runs away from school, but he carries the environment of the school around with him all the time. It's an inner element that's always there.

With this film were you talking about the mood in Iran at that time?

Indirectly. It's impossible not to refer to it—everything is related to it. Even now similarities between this time and that time still exist. I believe that no real change has occurred. It's only appearances that have changed.

"Breaktime" is my unfinished film. It had a much longer script. At the end of the script, there was a political, anti-American message. The child was supposed to take the ball of an American child and run away. In that period this kind of film was the fashion. I had approval for the film but I didn't finish it. Now I'm very happy that I didn't. Later I understood what a mistake it would have been.

Did you shoot the ending and not use it?

No, I didn't shoot it because I realized that it didn't fit. I realized that their beautiful relationship would provide a much better ending to the film. At that time Kanoon followed a political position that said we couldn't talk about the relationship between Iran and the US. It's necessary to say that, in fact, Kanoon was created so that leftists and political prisoners could work there and that it was under the supervision of Farah, the Shah's wife. That was the situation. We had some political cartoons made there, and fortunately they're forgotten now.

So you got approval to have this anti-American ending, but then you left it out because there was a policy change?

No, no. The ending hadn't been approved.

A friend of mine wrote an article about those days in Iran, and he mentioned that my film didn't satisfy anyone: neither the anti-Americans nor the pro-Americans. No one. Not even the producers. As I mentioned, I wanted to have helicopter shots in this film. For this reason, Farah got the Shah's helicopter. And the Shah kept asking me to show him the film. Finally, it was shown to him: the Shah yawned a couple of times, then scratched himself and left. Our producer said that the Shah didn't like the film. Nobody liked the film, except for four or five people. One was Bahram Beyzai, he said it was a good film. Personally, I never knew which film was good and which one was bad.

I think maybe the Shah was expecting to see something like the film The Lovers' Wind.*

I had used helicopter shots in the film, but even after seeing it, the Shah couldn't say where those shots were. So I took them out. The helicopter shots were when the kids were leaving school. It was a really beautiful shot: when school was just over and all the children poured into the street. But I couldn't see if all the children were waving to the helicopter.

---

* The French documentary *The Lovers' Wind* (1978), an airborne tour of Iranian landscapes by "The Red Balloon" director Albert Lamorrise, was a popular hit in Iran.

Experience
(56 mins., B&W, 1973)

Based on a story (and co-scripted) by Amir Naderi, this slice of a 14-year-old boy's life follows his efforts to fend for himself in the big city, working as a tea server and assistant in a photographer's studio, running errands and, briefly, exchanging glances with a pretty middle-class girl. With no music and little dialogue, and distinguished by its darkly elegant compositions, the film offers an impressionistic meditation on adolescent solitude.

Cheshire: Experience *came from a story by Amir Naderi. How did this film come about?*

Kiarostami: In those days, we had two kinds of filmmaking in Iran. We had a kind of Hollywood in Iran, and another kind of cinema which was very small. Naderi and I both agreed that we belonged to the small cinema. Therefore, I borrowed the story from him.

Experience does seem to resemble "Breaktime" in not having such a clear story. It's a beautifully-made film, and has a great feeling for the shop where the boy works and the streets around it, as well as the street where all the film theaters are.

I like the film, except for the last shot. I don't know, maybe it reminds me of the moment in "Bread and Alley," when the door is slammed and the dog is left out. In *Experience*, a girl opens the door and tells the boy that they don't want a servant. This means that he cannot enter. It's too melodramatic. I'd like to eliminate this last shot.

One thing I thought about was the relationship of the boy with his brother, whom he lives with. It's similar to in A Wedding Suit, *where the boy lives with his brother.*

I've never thought about that before. These things happen quite unconsciously—I don't decide them. For example, in this last shot of *Experience* I wasn't thinking about "Bread and Alley." Or, with *Where Is the Friend's House?*, I realized that after 15 years I had a dog, a boy, an old man, and an alley. After twenty years it came to my mind again. But there are always some similarities, you cannot prevent them.

In A Wedding Suit, *the relationship is much more complex. So, I was wondering if this earlier film gave you the idea that you could do something more with that kind of relationship.*

Right now as you say this, that does seem right. But I never before realized the similarity between the two films—I only just now realized it. That's why I insist on the fact that one shouldn't talk about only one film. I think the unconscious mind often has more value than the conscious mind.

The Traveler
(74 mins., B&W, 1974)

Kiarostami's first feature focuses on a boy in a provincial city so avid to get to Tehran to see a soccer match that he'll lie to adults and cheat other kids. A quest film that's also a study of youthful obsession, it's filmed in edgy B&W with a quiet energy that matches its hero's. Has an acridly ironic ending and one of the best performances by a child in Kiarostami's early work.

Cheshire: *How did you come to make* The Traveler*?*

Kiarostami: It was based on someone else's idea. Afterwards, I heard that he'd gotten the idea from a Spanish film, which concerns a boy who goes to watch a bullfight.

Is there anything specifically in the main character that comes from you, apart from general things like his passion?

The interior of the character comes from me, but I don't know what the motivation was to create such a character. I didn't like soccer, for instance. But what this film is talking about is longing, not soccer itself. What is still more important is the idea of not reaching goals: the point of our lives is to run after a goal without necessarily reaching it. You may not believe it but, for me, attaining something doesn't necessarily come with a feeling of achievement. After I received the Palme d'Or for *Taste of Cherry* I left the theater and went and put it in the hotel. Then Amir Naderi and I went for a walk on the beach. He asked me: "What are you feeling?" I said: "Nothing." So, you do reach your goal, you see the soccer match, but it doesn't deeply enter your heart. It stays outside of you—you become a part of the audience. You see a man

with glasses who goes on stage, they give him a Golden Palm, he says a few words in horrible French, and then comes down.

In The Traveler *did you give the child actor a detailed instruction about how to play the scene, or did you just give him his lines and some sort of explanation, such as expressing anger?*

I needed a child who loves soccer, so I searched the neighborhoods where children played it. And that's where I found him. When I found him he'd just had a terrible fight with his friend. His friend wanted to stop the soccer game and leave, but he insisted that he stay and play. He wanted a chance to beat his friend's team because they had just scored. On the whole I realized that he had extraordinary energy. It meant nothing to him that we went to him and asked him to act in a film. The only thing that was important to him was winning the soccer game.

I used his energy during the film. I knew what would make him happy and what would make him angry—knew how to push his buttons. I was familiar with his behavior, with his ups and downs, and knew what his desire was. With this particular information, I tried to create feeling in him. I never told him to "come and do this in front of the camera." I knew how to create a certain mood in him because I knew him well, and I only gave him the dialogue once we were at the shooting location. I never tell an actor how to feel and never talk to an actor about his other feelings. I plant the feeling in the actor the night before or one hour before shooting. They do say their dialogue according to my orders, but the feeling is up to them.

Tell me specifically about how you directed the scene where the boy is beaten.

I had an agreement with him. I told him that in that particular sequence we had to beat him up. I asked him what he wanted in exchange and he said he wanted a ball. So, we bought him a ball and a sports jersey. He then told the principal to beat him up harshly without any compassion.

So he directed the scene?

That's what I'm saying. In fact, he thought that if he wasn't beaten he wouldn't get what he'd asked for. For me, the first test of whether or not we could work with him was to see if he had a sense of responsibility. This is very important, because otherwise you cannot work with children. It's much more difficult when they resist you.

Which town is the film set in?

Originally it was supposed to be in Ghazvin, because the road between Tehran and Ghazvin is flat. For this reason, I thought it would be more believable if he went from Ghazvin to Tehran. There are no mountains on the way, and no bridges and no tunnels. I remember the first time I crossed through a tunnel to the other side: I had the feeling that I'd lost all my loved ones. That was the feeling I had about tunnels and this was the only road where there were no tunnels. But, when I went there, the accent of the Ghazvini people wasn't pleasant. There are many dirty jokes about that region. My story was tragic, so I didn't want to stimulate laughter. When I couldn't film it there, I went down that road and found myself in Malayer. Upon my arrival, I encountered a boy; his ball was on the road and he came to pick it up. So, it happened right there.

So that's where you made the film?

Yes. I made the film there, in Malayer.

And where is that?

It's toward the south of Iran, in Lorestan.

Are all the people in the film from that place?

Yes, all of them. Interestingly, it was my first experience of simultaneous sound recording on set.

Was this the first film shot like that in Iran?

Before that, one film was shot with simultaneous sound recording. Ebrahim Golestan's *The Brick and the Mirror* (1964) was made like that. He also used a Mitchell camera. Golestan had his own personal studio and a blimped Mitchell camera. I shot this film with an Arriflex, but it wasn't a blimped Arriflex. The cameraman was under the quilt, and our camera didn't have a synchronizing wire. He had an Uher, a regular Uher tape recorder, and when I returned to Tehran, everyone was worried that I wouldn't be able to fix the problem because the camera and the tape recorder were not in-sync during shooting. The shooting of the film took forty days, but the editing of the sound took four months.

I'm surprised it didn't take longer than that. It's a very difficult thing to do.

It was totally incredible. But, when I went to the location, I realized that this film should be shot with simultaneous sound recording or not be shot at all.

Tell me about the reaction to The Traveler—*was it good? Were you pleased? Was it seen in Iran and overseas?*

The Traveler was one of my best films. It was praised by audiences, critics, everyone. In reality, even those who still don't recognize me as a filmmaker would tell me that I've made one good film, and that's *The Traveler*.

Well it came out in a period, 1973-74, when there was a whole explosion of exciting new films.

I don't remember exactly. But it's possible to find out from the catalogues what films were made at Kanoon in that year.

I've a year-by-year list of films and that year was particularly strong.

What is interesting about Kanoon is that I think all filmmakers that went to Kanoon made their best films there. It's because of the extraordinary management of the head of Kanoon in those days [Lili Amir Arjomand]. She trusted us extraordinarily. That's why when outside filmmakers such as Amir Naderi, Bahram Beyzai, and Shahpoor Gharib, the director who made the *Wooden Pistols* and is now a mainstream director, came to Kanoon, they made their best films there. There were people who were not filmmakers and they came to Kanoon, experimented, and made films. It's something that doesn't exist now at all. In reality, there's no one in today's system who loves cinema. Those people are more like controlling agents than people who appreciate art. Trust doesn't exist anymore. I think that if the world is paying attention to Iranian cinema, it's related to those days at Kanoon. And I'm not passing any judgment whatsoever about the Pahlavi regime or the Islamic Republic. I'm only remembering the trust of a fine manager and her extraordinary management. I'm talking about trust, nothing could be more constructive than trust and confidence.

Was she the head of Kanoon from the time you came there?

No. She was the head before then.

So she was there from before you, and then until the Revolution?

Yes. She was there about six or seven years before me. This is where I'll say one should begin from a detail and then approach the entire picture. I cannot begin by comparing two systems: I start by comparing two people and then can approach the two systems.

What happened to her?

She left Iran. I've heard she lives in New York, but we've no connection.

What was the budget for The Traveler*?*

It was the minimum. I can say with certainty: no filmmaker has ever made cheaper films than my films. Do you know what the reason was? I had infinite resources at Kanoon because of trust. It was like a sea; there was a sea of budget for work. The reason that those films were made with such little money was that there was a budget for me as plentiful as the sea, but I'd only take a bowl out of it. Again, it was all about trust.

Kanoon and its filmmakers were like a totally separate, secluded island from the main body of Iranian cinema. It was both dependent on Iranian cinema and at the same time completely independent from it. Cinema outside of Kanoon controlled the box office and made money. They had their own organization, they met among themselves. So we didn't have much communication with them, and children's films especially didn't have many fans. With a lot of difficulty we found only one theater that would show our films on Friday mornings. So the cinema of Kanoon was an independent cinema, and its filmmakers, like me, were also separated. If you had asked anyone to name ten filmmakers at that time, I surely wouldn't have been on that list. Perhaps even if there was a list of twenty people I wouldn't have been one of them. Children's films were not taken seriously at all.

But The Traveler *isn't a film for children, right?*

It was included in the same category. When our colleagues saw the film, they took it seriously, but the category was still different.

Were you aware of what other filmmakers were doing?

I followed their works more than they followed mine.

"So Can I"
(4 mins., color, 1975)

The first of Kiarostami's films made for, rather than about, children was an experiment in combining live action and animation, done in collaboration with animator Nafiseh Riahi. As two schoolboys watch animated views of animals' actions, such as kangaroos jumping, fish swimming, etc., one boy (played by Riahi's son Kamal) says, "I can too," and imitates the actions. The music is sprightly, the mood fun. The second boy is Kiarostami's son Ahmad.

Cheshire: *The short film "So Can I" features your son Ahmad Kiarostami in his debut in a supporting role. This is the first film that seems to be for kids, as opposed to the previous ones which were about them.*

Kiarostami: It's for kids but, in my opinion, the idea is still intellectual. The concept is for adults. When you look at the film it's childish, because of the music, because of the animation, because of the acting. It was one of the experiments that I did at Kanoon. We really were just experimenting. For example, in this film I experimented with mixing animation and live actors. There was a woman at Kanoon who did animation and who had a child the same age as Ahmad. She did the animation and it was very experimental.

It was a collaboration with her?

Yes, I did the live part and she did the animation part.

What was her name?

Nafiseh Riahi. She'd done a number of good animations. In my opinion, animation begs more attention. Because some of these animated films have great qualities, they're very modern. It's very strange, but it appears we had a revolution only to eliminate animated films. Everything is as it was before; the only thing that's gone is animation. They told us not to work on animation. The Revolution of 1979 was an anti-animation revolution.

Did you do animations? Were you interested in animation as a graphic artist?

No, cartoons generally make me angry.

Why?

I can't understand why. Especially cartoons with human characters who talk—I don't understand at all why they make these. Animation should begin where humans cannot do the job. It should be a dream. But the world of animation is too often like real life. I can tell you a secret, and that's that I don't even like Walt Disney's animations.

"Two Solutions for One Problem"
(5 mins., color, 1975)

A simple moral tale that seems to prefigure *Where Is the Friend's House?*: Two young schoolboys are friends until Dara returns Nader's notebook torn and Nader retaliates in kind, setting off an escalating battle that leads to destruction of property and physical injury. In the second solution, Dara realizes his offense and repairs the notebook, preserving the peace and the friendship. Shot mostly in close-ups with a narrator drolly chronicling the action.

Cheshire: *The same year you made "So Can I," you also made "Two Solutions for One Problem," a film that concerned children.*

Kiarostami: I personally like this film, but only to a certain extent. I see the simplicity of its narration as being a little too close to early films, the silent era films. The camera is often fixed. It's a complicated story that's presented in a simple way. The story I acquired from Ahmad when he was going to school.

So Ahmad and his friend tore up each other's notebooks?

Yes. This is the film that satisfies me most as a "children's film." I think it has enough artistic quality for an art film, and, at the same time, is totally understandable for children. This gives it a distinguished simplicity.

And this is the first film where you have an either/or situation, as you do, for example, later in "Orderly or Disorderly."

Again, I can say both yes and no. [*Laughs*] I can say that it has one person in a good and bad situation, not one good person and one bad person. It's like in real life; each person has the potential to be good or bad. And that's how I view the subject. Maybe that's why this film had a great amount of impact on me: every time there was a problem, I'd think that I had two solutions. Which was the better one? With this paradigm, it's easy to understand that one solution leads to breaking and tearing, and the other doesn't. It's a film that one can watch every morning before leaving home, because people deal with this problem every single day. Sometimes the problems are very difficult, and sometimes they're much easier. The subject is very useful, and it's not abstract.

Was it your idea that it be shown to kids so that they could understand that there are different solutions to problems? Was this film screened in schools?

No, unfortunately not very often. These films usually didn't have a place to be shown. Maybe the best place was on TV, but the television industry had its own problems with Kanoon. Every institution worked for itself. TV preferred to buy Japanese films very cheaply and show them instead. But this kind of film would have been ignored anyway.

The film did win a grand prize at a New Mexico festival. I think it was the first or second international prize that I received from outside of Iran. It gave me a lot of self-confidence. To a certain extent, it was also an answer to the Iranian critics, who preferred complexity and abstraction in art. During those years there were many filmmakers who had studied in the West and who made complicated films.

Was there no mechanism for showing films like this in schools?

No. Sometimes they were shown, but the system itself didn't have the capacity. Big, commercial films made outside of Iran for children—those films with big budgets that entertain the audience and make them laugh—naturally garnered more attention. In those days, as was often the case, many of the filmmakers who made films for children made them so that the child could take their parents and grandparents to the cinema. But this kind of film is the kind that makes me yawn, and it's not for those who want to see a *film*.

A Wedding Suit
(59 mins., color, 1976)

In a tri-level shopping arcade, a teenage boy who works for a tailor is besieged by two other boys who want to borrow a new suit to wear on a social outing before it's turned over to its owner. One of the most accomplished and intricately plotted of Kiarostami's Kanoon films, this sharply observed drama contains suspense, satire, an undercurrent of violence, even a magic show.

Cheshire: *Let's talk about* A Wedding Suit. *It's one of my favorite films of yours.*

Kiarostami: I'm very glad. It's one of the films that isn't seen by most people.

I think the craft of this movie is extraordinary. It's also very subtle. It took me a second viewing to understand that it's about child abuse.

It seems that they themselves are unaware they're abused—when we look at them from the outside, we realize what a bad situation they're in. This is why we have to respect children. I mean, children are better than us because they cope with difficulties better. They've more energy for living than we do and tolerate life with a great amount of realism. And they know how to enjoy life in bad conditions. This is what I like a lot about this film. As I've said, we comprehend this very bad situation more than the children themselves do.

I like the sequence where the child wears the borrowed suit. Feeling that he must enjoy it as much as possible, he goes to a café where a magic act is going on and sits in the spotlight

so everyone can see him. The magician pulls his shirt off—I like this moment a lot. The child is left with the suit jacket directly on his bare skin. There's no distance left—he can embrace the object of his desires without any interference. It's like something that happened in *Close-Up* with Hossein Sabzian, when he rode the motorcycle in close physical proximity to Makhmalbaf, his favorite director. Reality and dream occur simultaneously; reality and dream become one.

Where did the idea for A Wedding Suit *come from?*

I don't remember exactly, but I know that one day someone told me about three friends who had bought a brown suit together. They put their money together and bought a suit, and each day one of them would wear it. The idea came from this story.

Why did you make it a one-hour film rather than a feature?

I made it without considering the length. I didn't have good business sense.

If it had been a feature, it would have had the chance to reach a bigger audience.

Yes, I know. If it were now, I'd add to the story and make it longer. Not for the sake of the box office, but because more people would get a chance to see it. Film is an art and should be presented in a way that allows large audiences to see it. I think if my films could write to me, some would write: "Why did you make me so short?" My films have a right to complain, and this film would blame me by saying: "I'm in limbo." It would say that nobody sees it because of its length.

We have a poet by the name of Nima Youshij. He was a very famous poet and he always wrote his poems on the back of cigarette packs. These poems were very good, and if it weren't for a number of people who gathered and organized them, they would have been lost now. Jalal Ale Ahmad wrote an article about him in which he expressed his anger toward Youshij's way of working. He said that: "Presenting the work is a vital part of art, and must be done in a way that allows enough people to see it. The task of exposing the artwork is on the shoulder of the artist."

So you do think the one-hour length kept people from seeing it?

Yes. This happened to all the one-hour films. In reality medium length isn't good. Films should be either short or long.

One of the subtle touches in the film is that when we see the boy riding to work in an early scene, he's rubbing his nose. And it's only much later that we come to understand the reason for this—he's been beaten.

What is interesting for me in this film is that, although he's a bully and a villain, in one specific moment he becomes innocent. I'm talking about when the magician pours Coke in the suit jacket's pocket. At this moment, when the boy is simply worried about the jacket, we see he's not a bad guy at all. Now that we're talking about him, I realize he resembles Sabzian. He's wearing a garment that's not his: he is a fake. He wants to show off, much as Sabzian did.

One interesting thing is that the film at first seems to be about these two boys, and it's only later that we realize that it's really about the third boy. This is subtle and very unusual; most films tell you who the main character is right away.

This is also the case in *The Report*. At the beginning of the film, we don't understand who the main character is. The film runs for ten, fifteen minutes, and we still don't know who the main character is.

There's also a fourth boy, for whom the suit is made. And there's a great scene with him and his mother: in just about two minutes you can see so many things about their relationship. And there's a strong indication of the Shah's time, in that the mother has these liberal ideas. She wants the child to choose, but he chooses an old type of suit.

That child is the one who was in the film "Bread and Alley."

He's great too. His performance is just wonderful.

Now he has a suitcase store on the square, down the block.

The film also gives you a picture of the class structure in the Shah's time, and the film in some ways is about that too.

Yes, exactly.

The other thing I like is where most of the story takes place—that arcade, with its different levels.

It's a working-class area. I especially like that there's so much conversation going on. The sound in the scene when he follows the other boy creates a lot of suspense. We worked a lot on the sound for that scene. There's the sound of distant music, which isn't clear at all: it sounds like scratching. It's very Hitchcockian. I mention the sound because, for me, it bears the same importance as the picture itself.

And the magician onstage, is he someone you found?

Yes, he was a magician but the magic act he performed—pulling up the shirt and pouring the Coke in the jacket pocket—was created by me.

Does the arcade still exist?

That place is still there. A month ago, I was passing by there with Bahman and I showed it to him. We constructed the little pool for the film. Now they've filled it with soil and planted flowers in it. But the rest of the arcade is as it was then.

Where is it?

It's in Shah Abad. I'll take you there and get you a good *abgoosht*.

I like the way you use light in the film, especially the early morning light. It's beautifully filmed. Who shot it?

The cinematographer was Firooz Malekzadeh, who's now in Australia working as a taxi driver. He is the one who shot *The Traveler* as well. And [Amir Naderi's] *The Runner* also. He was one of the best cameramen in Iranian cinema. Although he was illiterate, he had a great feeling for light.

"The Colors"
(15 mins., color, 1976)

Ostensibly a film for children, this picturebook essay about the range of hues that brighten our world has the air of a delightfully playful formalistic exercise. As a narrator runs though the colors one by one, Kiarostami shows us where each appears in nature and human life (which occasions some great views of pre-Revolutionary consumer culture in Iran). Of course there's a little boy, who gets to fantasize about being a race car driver in one memorable sequence.

Cheshire: *Let's move on to another short, "The Colors" from 1976. What do you remember about it?*

Kiarostami: I made this film for children, and they were indeed very entertained by it.

It has some of the qualities of advertising films and TV commercials of that period. You did work in those areas. Is there a connection?

No. I wasn't doing commercials for TV at that time, but I knew that children really like rhythm. If you want kids to see a film you have to have rhythm in it. The best films for children are commercials. When Ahmad and Bahman were little, even when they were only six months or one year old, they would stop eating when commercials began. They wouldn't turn their head until the commercial was over. They didn't get the message, they didn't buy the merchandise, but they enjoyed the rhythm. And, in this film, I incorporated messages for them using colors. For example, they have to stop at the red light and cross the street on the striped pedestrian walkway. And other things like this. But what seems most important are rhythm and colors.

"Tribute to the Teachers"
(17 mins., color, 1977)

An assignment from the Ministry of Education, this documentary from the last years of the Pahlavi dynasty includes interviews with officials who predictably praise teaching as sacred, noble and honorable. The teachers themselves are less starry-eyed; one speaks of ungrateful students and the job's poor pay. The contrasting views express Kiarostami's interest in education while registering some of his reservations about how it's practiced.

Cheshire: *I want to ask you about a film called "Tribute to the Teachers," which I understand no longer exists. Is that right?*

Kiarostami: It was an assignment from the Ministry of Education. I made the film and they were supposed to show it in a big venue, in the presence of the Shah, on teacher's day. I made the film and then the Minister of Education came to see it. He told me to cut out one scene from the film. When I asked why, he said that he was sure the Shah wouldn't like it. It was a documentary scene: a number of people who had come to become teachers were gathered there for the contest of entering the school as teachers, and there was a large number of women wearing black chadors. I said: "Since I shot this in a documentary fashion and there's no interference from my own personal ideas, and it's the truth, I cannot take it out. But since I was commissioned to make the film and you have paid for it, you can take the scene out—that's not a problem." What's interesting is that he said that if I wasn't happy with their decision he wouldn't take it out, but the only thing was that he couldn't present the film to the Shah. So we agreed not to show it, and

they didn't show it. Now that I think about it, I realize that the Minister of Education did the right thing. It wasn't appropriate for him to censor the film. He understood that he shouldn't do something that I wasn't happy with.

It's at this point that I want to emphasize that I cannot compare the two time periods [pre-Revolution and post-Revolution] with each other. During the Shah's regime, despite all the negatives, I can still pay attention to a good experience with a good person. That's why I cannot say one regime is good and the other is bad. Things have to be examined piece by piece, in detail.

Did the film disappear at that point? Was it ever shown?

No, never. Because if they want to show it now they would certainly say the opposite and want to take out the women without veils. [*Laughs*] The truth is that both types of women lived in this society then. And, in my opinion, these two groups still exist now.

What happened to the film?

I don't know. It should be at Kanoon.

You think it still exists?

It should still be there. Anyway, even if certain films like this one exist they're not allowed to be shown. *A Wedding Suit* is forbidden because of a scene where the boy comes and looks at a girl who's up there and she waves to him; then they climb up the stairs together. In the magic show scene, the magician's assistant doesn't wear a scarf—that would also cause problems now.

It was your first documentary, in a sense.

Yes, if you look at it that way. I always said *Fellow Citizen* was my first documentary, but I'd totally forgotten about this other one. We shot it in a documentary style and with exemplary teachers who have dedicated their entire life to education. It's about the value of teaching. And there's also another story in the film: a teacher gets very old and a younger teacher comes in to take his place.

The Report
(112 mins., color, 1977)

The rare early Kiarostami film made outside of Kanoon, and one of the most downbeat of his features, this adult drama concerns a civil servant besieged on two fronts: he's accused of taking bribes, and his marriage is collapsing. Full of pre-Revolutionary disquiet, the film features future star Shohreh Aghdashloo as the wife.

Cheshire: *Your next film was your second feature,* The Report. *It obviously has nothing to do with Kanoon. How did you come to make it?*

Kiarostami: Yes, this was my first film outside of Kanoon. I made it after Parviz Kalantari, the painter, recommended I make it. I told him the narrative, which was based on a true story. Well, three true stories. I took the three experiences and put them all together into one story. The lead character was a mixture of these three people. I took the job from one story, the social class from another, and the family life from the third—the combination of all these people was the lead character. I was one of those people, one of those three. The main character was very close to me, so I made it.

You mean you identified with this character?

Without intention. I didn't know how close he was to me until the film was finished. Everyone who saw it told me I'd taken that side of the character from myself. I haven't watched the film from beginning to end, not even once. Never. And although I knew I could find a copy of it very easily, I never even tried until four years ago. I do have a copy now, but haven't watched it.

It's a very powerful movie emotionally.

But it drives me crazy.

What about the production, was there anything unusual about it besides the use of sync sound?

The person who worked on the film's sound didn't have experience with synchronized sound. He did something very strange: when we shot a scene several times and decided that the last one was good, he'd already erased the previous takes. He didn't know anything, and I didn't know much either. But, now that I look back on it, I think the sound work was good. I mean, for an Arriflex camera the sound work was good enough.

It also looks great. The camera is mobile.

Yes. It was the cameraman's first film too. He hadn't done anything before this. He'd only worked on short films, and had never done lighting, for example.

I know that in the case of some directors, before they shoot a film they'll show certain films to their cinematographers and ask them to shoot the scenes accordingly. Do you do that?

No.

Although The Traveler *and* The Report *can be seen as very different films, they do share many commonalities. In some senses, they can both be read as critiques of the Iranian character. Would you accept this description?*

No. I don't intentionally criticize the Iranian character. Sometimes one can approach a broad idea, but from a small detail. While I don't completely disagree with what you say, I didn't intentionally set out to do that.

It's something like a puzzle. We made a puzzle and I just tried to put the pieces together. When they're all put together and you look at it from a distance, it seems like a complete scene. I absolutely refrain from making critical or political films but, I think, at the same time there's no film that isn't critical or political. But, when you set out to look at the problem from a social or political point of view, in my opinion, your film risks becoming an academic essay.

I agree. The film isn't superficial, in that you are talking about character rather than sociology or politics.

What I'm trying to say is that issues such as politics and sociology exist within a film regardless. But, if you decide to approach something from a theoretical standpoint, there's danger of the theory becoming the dominant form. The protagonist in *The Report* is a citizen, he's living in a system, and he is affected by what is happening. He belongs somewhere. Therefore, if you closely study his character, you realize that he's the product of a certain social life and political situation. But, in my opinion, the first encounter between the two main characters is a very close and friendly one between two people. Like us. We don't really consciously think about where we are now. We talk about the same things though, and the only difference is our point of view.

Let me approach the same matter from another angle. Someone said to me recently that the difference between pre- and post-Revolutionary films is that there are no bad guys in the latter. It's funny, but there's a truth to it. In The Traveler *and* The Report, *the main characters are both good and bad. They do have a strong element of bad, which makes the viewer stand back and not completely identify with them—the audience can adopt a critical attitude towards them. It seems to me that this is different from your films after the Revolution.*

Let me say something about the Revolution, although it might be a little dangerous. If you remove the date of production from my films, I think it's very hard to say which was made before the Revolution, and which afterwards. If you shuffle my films like a deck of cards, I think it would be nearly impossible to put them back in chronological order. It's like palm reading. By closely observing the films, we realize that there hasn't been a revolution. I don't believe at all that a revolution can have an impact on art, at least in a short time.

I didn't become a revolutionary person overnight. There was an instance here in Iran when I was taken to see the Metro. They interviewed me and asked me to go into the tunnels to film the construction developments. The goal was to show the Iran of today. Without rejecting them and with a feeling of pride as a citizen, I said: "No, my material is human beings, not tunnels. If people come and go in these tunnels for twenty, thirty years and if I see the effect of this new way of using the tunnel on people's faces, on their emotions and relationships, that's what I need to show. My camera won't go downstairs, my camera will stay upstairs, and if someone comes up from the tunnel, I'll understand from the expression on his face that something has happened."

Change takes a long time to happen. How can someone expect me to show change in my films? My job isn't to make documentaries or political films on command. For me it's difficult to show these changes, unless there's a change in myself because of my age. For example, at the time of *The Report*, it's obvious that my life was bitter. I was in a dark mood. And then in the following films, like *Where Is the Friend's House?*, which marked the beginning of the second phase of my career, there was a change in my personal life. This change led me to make that film.

I think the main characters in both The Traveler *and* The Report *have a mixture of good and bad. The bad is strong enough that you resist identifying with them, which leads you to look at them critically.*

I don't look at it that way.

But the main character in The Report *is such an obnoxious, annoying character from the very beginning, when he breaks the glass of the old man serving tea. You can't sympathize with him.*

But I don't judge my characters. If I don't decide to make this character black or white, negative or positive, then the audience will also not judge. I did struggle with him, hate him, feel pity for him. If we get truly close to people we'll find both good and evil in them. We should look at people as if they are naked. In reality it's we who dress them with good or evil. Sometimes we choose to put the good garment on them, and sometimes we choose the evil garment.

I agree that, in *The Report*, that person wasn't a very pleasant person. And he wasn't a hero. But, he also wasn't an anti-hero.

I believe characters should make an impression on us, so we can find similarities between them and us. For me, the sign of this is when we recognize an action or a behavior that also exists in us.

When did you write and shoot The Report*?*

I wrote it in 1976. In fact, it was at Bahman Farmanara's suggestion, because he had a production company outside of Iran. That company was supposed to co-produce several films. There was one with Orson Welles, but because of the Revolution it was canceled. When I wrote the synopsis for Farmanara, I didn't expect him to accept it. Then I found out that he'd told his secretary to ask me to write the screenplay. It was one of those scripts that I wrote very easily, in one week. I remember that he brought up some concerns, such as how we could possibly find a two-year-old child who'd be able to say the dialogue. I replied that I didn't know, but we had to try. And we did find a child who said all the dialogue exactly the way it was written, full of feeling.

How did you get that child to perform?

I'm really amazed by that performance. It gives me a lump in my throat. I always say: a director can only do one part of the job, the rest must just happen—there's no other way. You have to create the situation and wait until it happens. Good films are the ones in which something like this happens, moments that you can't repeat. There are no second takes for them and you can't see them in another film. I think this is what gives value to a film. Some films only have the value of being well made. In such cases, if you try, you can make it again, perhaps even a little better. If you enhance the technical aspects, you can make it better for sure. But, in my opinion, a shot depends on a metaphysical element: it's a moment that just happens. During the moment when the child is crying and the parents are hitting each other there were seventeen other people in the room. But it feels as if everything—the camera and the seventeen people—have disappeared. The feeling of loneliness experienced by this child is completely felt. The child was friendly with everyone—she loved everyone during the filming—but when we started to shoot this two-minute scene, she acted very naturally. We thought she might come to one of us behind the camera, but she didn't. She just stood there all alone.

It's amazing to me that a child could do that.

In the dialogue, her mother asked her to put on a dress so that they could go out. Her father just stood there. Of course he wasn't her real father, he was part of the cast, but she looked at him and said: "I want Daddy to come with us too." She was crying, she wanted her dad to go along with them. She looked in our exact direction and with intense feeling said: "Let's take Daddy with us." Life is very natural, and such things happen. But when there are seventeen people and a camera, a black monster right in front of her, and someone is standing there with the boom, the feeling might be destroyed. I thought she would've asked for the whole crew to go with her, not just the father.

As you said, there are perhaps three levels to this story. Regarding the work level, which we see first, was that supposed to be specifically about this kind of bureaucracy or about what was going on generally in society at that time?

That came from a person who once shared his story with me. He talked to me about his work, how he was accused of taking bribes, and that he had a terrible life. All this was the true story of that person. But he didn't have family problems; we added family problems to the story. I added them to his story very deliberately.

The way this guy treats the old man serving tea I think tells you a lot about him.

That story about breaking the cup is from my own memory, from my first day working in an office for the highway patrol when I was nineteen or twenty years old. There was nothing important in the breaking of the cup in itself. What I found important was that I couldn't adequately convey to the people around me how sweet and sensitive the story was: I was charged for breaking an unbreakable cup! The cup actually broke! I asked the man how much the cup was, and he said it cost two tomans. I was surprised it was so expensive, so I asked him the reason, and he said it was because the cup was unbreakable. We've that same exact dialogue in the film. The character asks why he was charged that much, and the other man replies that it's because he broke an unbreakable cup. The character then asks: "If it was unbreakable, why did it break?" The fact that I couldn't make anyone around me understand that point made me feel very lonely among them.

But, in the film, I think the feeling is very different. You feel sorry for the old man because of his age and his position, and you feel the main character is being a jerk for treating him badly.

I think, in this kind of story, if you don't waste your attention on unimportant things, you can understand the point of the film. Paying attention to secondary characters prevents you from focusing on the main character before getting to know those other characters. I mean, let's say a bunch of people set out together and one of them distinguishes himself little by little. It's like going to a party where many people are introduced to you who you haven't met before, and gradually one of them stands out. But this takes time, you have to get acquainted. At the start of the film we're getting acquainted, but this introduction must happen gradually. This is a kind of "character dimmer," so that we can gradually get close to the main character. We don't judge from the beginning whether he's a good person or a bad person. I think the main character, Mr. Firoozkoohi, is liked by some and hated by others. Sometimes they like him, sometimes they don't like him.

I think viewers are put off by him from early on, because of the way he behaves.

But gradually they also come to sympathize with him. Perhaps not very much, but you do make a connection with him. Before realizing whether you like him or dislike him, you make a connection with him.

One thing is that he seems guilty of taking the bribe. The guy who comes in and accuses him talks about being a good Muslim and so on, but from the way Mr. Firoozkoohi reacts he gives the impression that he's guilty.

That's why I think the audience should be "behind" the work, so they don't decide too quickly who's good and who's bad. A friend of mine told me that when he went to the movies as a child with his father, if they were late and hadn't seen the beginning of the film, he would ask his father to tell him who the bad guy was and who the good guy was. He wanted everything to be clear and to know whether the protagonist was good or bad. He did the same thing with TV films. When he got home late and saw a film was halfway through, he would ask the same thing. However, I believe that a film should keep you from knowing who the good and bad guys are until the end. The film should pull you in deeper. This is true in real life, too. Bahman is my witness when I talk about my friends. One day I may say that this person is a great person, and the next day I may say that this same person is a very nasty person. This is the truth about people: they aren't just black or white.

Besides this guy being guilty or innocent, were you trying to show something about corruption in the government at that time?

I didn't try to show corruption. It's not my job to do so but, when you want to get close to a person's soul, we do see that there are temptations around him. It's very important to me to show the temptation of a person toward both good and evil. Very important. And this isn't about Iranian history. It's about human history. It goes back to Adam and Eve. They were told: "This is good, but don't eat it." What is important is creating the temptation. Balzac said something like: "If you resist temptation, it's not always a sign of your strength. It's a sign that the temptation is weak." I believe that this issue is always approachable, in any language and for any nationality. Something that's attractive to you but has been forbidden according to ethics should be ignored; an ethical obstacle blocks it. And this, in my opinion, has a tragic nature which could be the essence of any art. This is the foundation of drama.

The depiction of the couple's marriage is very complex. I was struck by the scene where the husband won't tell the wife that a colleague's wife has had a baby that's a boy, though he knows that's the case. It seems to indicate something about his own troubles.

He's caught in such a difficult relationship that anything can create an explosion. In Iran, there's this reprehensible idea that a woman's first child should be a boy. Perhaps they prefer the same for the second and third as well. The root of this goes back to ancient Persian culture. That's why when his wife wants to give a girl's dress to the other couple, he doesn't want to say that the child is a boy. He wants to maintain the home's peaceful atmosphere. It's like striking a match: he thinks that he shouldn't light that match.

At the beginning of the film, the protagonist lets slip that something is wrong. Therefore, the news that something is wrong causes us to want to know what happened. This is what I mentioned before: it's the "dimmer." We mention first that something is wrong and then show the damage itself. This specifically is meant as a sign of respect to the kind of audience that likes to discover on its own. When you discover something on your own, you become one with the film. You get involved in order to discover what is happening between these two people. With only a sign, one finds a clue.

My favorite scene is the one on the street with the car, where both the husband and wife overreact, but they can't control the policeman and it's one of those situations where life overwhelms them. The whole way the scene is staged is amazing.

In reality, these details are signs. These details bring out the depth of the characters as well as their good relationship. But, you have seen the censored version.

Is that scene censored?

No. The scene from the night before. You haven't seen it. Ten minutes of the film, in bed.

In bed? Yes, someone told me the scene before the couple started making love was cut.

They cut the lovemaking scene because it's so bitter. They didn't cut it because of the bitterness; they cut it because of the lovemaking itself. If you saw this scene, you would see that in the lovemaking there existed signs of an explosive fight that would occur the following day. The scene prepares you for the fight. It was lovemaking that wasn't lovemaking at all. Therefore, even though there was some sort of desire in it, it triggered the domestic strife between the couple.

Does the footage that was taken out exist somewhere? Could there be a restored version?

No, it definitely doesn't exist. They destroyed the negative after the Revolution. The only thing that exists is this videotape. It's possible it's lying around somewhere, under a staircase, in terrible condition. But, even if it does still exist, it can't be a good copy.

There's no print of it?

No, Bahman Farmanara, the producer, tried hard to find it.

One thing about The Report *is that it uses longer scenes than your other films. I counted and there are only something like 15 scenes in the whole film.*

I didn't know that myself.

Really? You don't normally plan out the scenes?

No. Usually I don't have a habit of thinking about my scenes before shooting. And I don't have a habit of choosing my lenses or the length of my shots before going to location. So, since I do my decoupage right there on set, when I set up the camera, everything depends on the power of the image and the strength of the actors. I think it's very much like driving and shifting gears. Sometimes conditions force you to keep changing gears. Therefore, I believe that the rhythm of the film depends on the inner energy of the actors. The rhythm isn't given to the film from the outside. Each scene has a certain amount of power and energy—when you see that it's running low on energy, you change the position of the camera. That's why I can't predict how I'll shoot my films beforehand.

Was The Report *more scripted than* The Traveler? *It seems more scripted than many of your later films.*

This is a good point. It was. There was a professional producer working with me who wanted everything written beforehand. I never did it like this again. The production crew was a very large one, and it was my first professional feature film outside Kanoon, meaning that it wasn't a children's film. Therefore, I thought I had to equip myself better in every way. That's why *The Report* was written much more diligently and meticulously than my other films, and perhaps why I didn't enjoy making it as much.

I do always write down certain things while writing, or at least I've things in detail in my head. But, when shooting, I'm always ready for something new to happen, and am prepared to change my plans. If I shoot exactly what I've written it's very boring for me. Since *The Report*, whenever I write a film very meticulously, I can't make it. Then I give it to other people. [Alireza Raisian's] *The Journey* was one of the scripts that I wanted to film myself, but when I saw that everything was so precisely written, I lost the desire to make it. Also, [Ebrahim Forouzesh's] *The Key* falls into that same category. Usually, a three-page draft is ideal for me to start filming. Then I like to discover the rest day-by-day, on set. *Close-Up* didn't even have those three pages. *Through the Olive Trees* started with three pages, and I started *And Life Goes On* with just a short synopsis.

Both lead actors in The Report *were very, very good. Where did you find them?*

I looked for the male character for a long time. I was looking for him among well-known actors, as I was afraid to shoot a feature film with non-professional actors. But one day this man entered an elevator I was in. He was pale and talking about a fight that his friend had just been in, that he was also involved in. We were on the sixth floor, and by the time we reached the first floor I decided he was the actor for my film. When we got out we went to the street, and I proposed that he should be the main character in my film. This caused him to forget about the fight. Finding him happened as simply as that.

The female lead, Shohreh Aghdashloo, was the wife of one of my friends who's a modern painter. I hadn't met her but I told my friend to ask his wife to read the script, and said if she wanted to play the part she could play it. I knew that she liked to act but that she hadn't done anything. She was a model at that time. You might have a very good question now, which would be: "How could you give your lead part to someone you had never seen act?" This has a very private answer. If you want,

I'll tell it to you, but not here.

But both actors are very good in the film, very strong.

I agree and I especially think the man's acting was very sensitive. Both are very good, but his job was more difficult.

What happened to him?

He is now in America. He lives in LA, and I know that he doesn't have a job.

Another striking scene is near the end, where the man stops and goes in a bar and has a conversation but leaves the child outside. The viewer's mind is divided between these two things.

I think the interesting thing is that, at the climax of the scene when they fight and the child is crying, emotion also permeated the crew; so much so that we didn't have the strength to stay and film the scene. So we went out and took a break. This scene wasn't supposed to be at that point in the film. I switched around its placement as I thought that the crew's desire to leave the house at this emotional moment would be mirrored by the audience in the theater—they would also want to get out of there. It seemed to me that it was such an intense climax that the audience wouldn't be able to tolerate it anymore. I do want to provoke emotion, but there's a danger of people getting alienated from the film.

Therefore, in the next scene, the presence of the child in the car created a relationship between the two scenes. The child outside is, in fact, the tragic element of this story that's always with them. We never forget the child. And we don't forget the chaos and clamor inside the home either.

I think people can only tolerate drama to a certain extent. Afterwards there should be a silent moment so people can recharge. This is something special that's found in literature but not really in cinema. When a chapter ends in a novel half the page is blank, then there's another blank page after that, and then another chapter starts with a number. The reader at this point can decide to turn the book over and go to have a tea or go out. But cinema doesn't afford the audience this luxury. Literature is kind to its reader, but cinema isn't this way, it's not kind. There are films that don't let you relax—you hold onto the armrest constantly. This is a pressure put onto the audience. I think that one can add pauses at certain points in a film to give the viewer a break to relax a little. You can add some images into the film to indicate such a pause. In *Through the Olive Trees*, I did this technique a couple of times. The professionals would say this is when the film falls off. I like it when it falls off. I say the reason it falls off is for you to relax, like when in a book you look at a blank page and that gives you a break.

A little detail I liked is that in the final scene, which is very serious, there's a bit about the guy getting the doctor's parking space. It reminded me of John Ford films, where there's often a moment of humor even in the most serious scenes.

I think that's how it is. In real life there's always humor. It always exists. But when we're being serious it becomes more visible. For instance, in memorial services, there's always the possibility that something will cause people to laugh. Since we're in a specific, dramatic mood, humor is even more noticeable. A film or drama without any humor is absolutely meaningless.

Did The Report *come out to theaters? Was it in festivals?*

It was shown once, but right during the climax of the Revolution, when the Revolution was really taking shape. Iranian critics praised it a lot. But then the Revolution happened, and there was no chance of showing the film anymore. In fact, it was one of the films that was removed from the theater by the Revolution. After that, it wasn't screened anywhere. And its print was destroyed.

So it's never shown?

No.

"Solution"
(11 mins., color, 1978)

The rare Kanoon film that doesn't involve children, this unusual road movie was made as the Revolution approached and may have afforded Kiarostami a welcome escape from the capital. Shot amid spectacular mountain scenery north of Tehran, it shows a young man on a roadside with a tire, trying to get a ride. After several minutes of failure, he simply takes the tire and rolls it down the mountain, a lyrical visual journey that's accompanied by a triumphal score.

Cheshire: *Let's talk about "Solution."*

Kiarostami: The idea for the film is a combination of a personal experience with another event that I heard had happened in Germany: someone's tire was flat, and he stood in the expressway trying to hail a car for hours. Apparently, he did this for eleven hours, and then he set himself on fire. Then all the cars stopped, but it was too late. It happened on Christmas night, on one of the express highways in Cologne. This was shown on the news in Iran, so I combined my idea with it. The film was made with exactly three people: the soundman, the cameraman, and me. No four people, including the actor. It was a very enjoyable shoot. I can actually say that we were five, since the tire also became a character. It had an independent personality, and sometimes it didn't listen to us; it wasn't supposed to fall into the river, but it would fall in anyway. And then we were obliged to change the tire. It was really exciting.

It looks like a real professional actor, that tire.

The tire is as strong as Marlon Brando in front of the camera. It's utterly powerful, independent, and it does what it wants. Sometimes it's malformed.

Where did you film it? North of Tehran?

It's a combination of three or four roads. Yes one was the road to Galandowak, one was the road to Firoozkooh, and one the road to Chaloos.

"Jahan Nama Palace"

(30 mins., color, 1978)

This documentary depicts the elaborate four-year restoration of one building in the Niavaran Palace Complex in north Tehran, where the last Shah and his family resided. Narrated partly by young architect/designer Manijeh Torfeh, the film describes the efforts to integrate modern technology with restored traditional crafts, which involved 50 artisans imported from around Iran. Perhaps to offset the royal poshness, Kiarostami pauses to observe the workers' prayers.

Cheshire: *The next film is "Jahan Nama Palace."**

Kiarostami: I made this film in four years, during the reconstruction of an old palace. It was a palace where the Shah and his first wife Fawziah had lived.

Who commissioned it?

It was commissioned by Farah, the Shah's wife.

So it wasn't done through Kanoon?

No, it wasn't for Kanoon. But on the day it was finished the Revolution happened. I never saw a print of the film. But I know there's a print in Paris, and they're supposed to arrange a screening.

I heard it's now with the producer. Who was that?

---

* Since its rights are privately held, this film was not included in the 2019 Kiarostami restorations and U.S. retrospective.

Her name is Manijeh [Torfeh] Ghiai. She is an interior designer who lives in Paris. I saw her when I was last there. It's a film I really want to see, because I don't really remember anything about it. It must be something like thirty or forty minutes long.

And you shot it off-and-on for four years up until the Revolution?

As a matter of fact we only had a day of shooting every month, because of the reconstruction of the palace. It was the Niavaran Palace where the Shah lived. The upper floor was his office. Farah said that the Shah didn't have good memories of that place, because he'd lived there with his ex-wife. Farah wanted to change the architecture of that place in such a way that the Shah would forget his bad memories.

I was wondering why she would want a film of it if it had these bad associations.

That itself was also a good reason. They had started to change the palace entirely. My film was the explanation for the expenses, to show how much work was done there. I remember that there was a door that was boarded up. We saw someone push it and open it with a kick, and dust fell from the top. He came in and we saw that it was the Shah. He looked around a little and left.

So you saw the Shah during the making of your film?

Yes, he came for a moment. It was very interesting: there was a silence, and all of a sudden one of the workers said "Salam aleikum" in a very slang fashion. The Shah had dust on his clothes. This was the only time in those four years that he came downstairs, although his office was upstairs. In fact, the idea behind this film was basically explaining all those difficult phases of reconstruction, because the building had been transformed into a warehouse for gifts that came from foreign countries. When they emptied the place, they realized that everything was damp.

So the film was about the restoration rather than the building, per se? Did you finish it?

Yes, it was completed.

What happened to it then?

I didn't know what had happened but, when I saw Mrs. Ghiai, she told me that the new regime owned the film secretly and that three or four years after the Revolution, with much difficulty, she'd taken it out of Iran to Paris.

So it was never shown in Iran?

Nobody saw it, not even myself.

Case No. 1, Case No. 2
(47 mins., color, 1979)

Made in the spring of 1979, not long after the Shah's overthrow, this extraordinary film serves as a Rorschach blot for people in a revolutionary mindset. Kiarostami stages two versions of a classroom discipline situation (in one, a student tells on a troublemaker; in the other, seven students refuse to rat) and then has several adult authorities comment on the outcomes. The fascinating responses evoke conflicts between order and resistance.

Cheshire: *Case No. 1, Case No. 2 is an incredible film and such a document of a time.*

Kiarostami: You said something exceptional, because you can only make a film like this during a transition of power. I mean, at any other time it isn't possible.

I salute you for having the presence of mind to make the film when you did, because many people wouldn't have thought of the idea until five years later.

Although that wasn't my intention at the time, this film is a historical film. People who were caught by surprise at this specific moment in history helped to make the film. If I was to make it again with the same people, the same film wouldn't be made.

The other thing that's apparent in *Case No. 1, Case No. 2* is how the lower class, the illiterate class, has a tendency toward dictatorship. We interviewed the fathers, of which two were relatively educated and four were illiterate—the four who were illiterate voted for a dictatorial regime. They voted for power, all of them. From this we can easily understand certain things, certain values that we only come to realize are important later. All the people in this film later changed their mind— those who gained power—and it was power itself that destroyed them. None of them is in a position of power now. And one of them, Ghotzbadeh, was executed.

When exactly was it made?

I can guess the exact date by looking at how people are dressed. The shooting of the film began during the time of the Revolution [early 1979]. The day we went to the television station to conduct interviews, people stormed and occupied it. We shot some interviews with one person who was later executed: the head of the TV station at the time of the Shah, called Jafarian. When the Revolution happened the project stopped. Roughly three months after the Revolution, we went to the TV station to continue the interviews, and then realized this wouldn't be possible. So we put the project on hold for another three months, and I think on Nowrooz [Iranian New Year, the Spring equinox] of that year we started again. I remember interviewing Khalkhali and my colleagues were afraid of him. It was the height of the executions. He was executing many people, every day.*

So you started shooting the classroom parts before the Revolution and tried to do some interviews, but then stopped?

Yes, we'd shot the classroom scenes with a 16mm camera, so we could show them to people. In those days, film recording and viewing were not like they are today.

How long did it take to shoot those interviews?

Since it was all very well planned, I don't think it took more than one month.

Were some people wary, or refused to participate?

No, but they would put forth a lot of conditions. After we'd finished an interview, the Minister of Guidance told us not to use the interview. We promised him this and took out the film from the camera. He was the only one.

What's striking is that people seem to answer by responding to a preconceived idea, rather than the reality of the situation.

Exactly. Ghotbzadeh, who started the revolutionary television

---

* Sadegh Khalkhali, a Shia cleric who was named by Ayatollah Khomeini to head the Islamic Republic's Revolutionary Courts, became known as Iran's "hanging judge" for ordering the summary executions of countless prisoners.

agency, said that he wanted to "reveal things" while it was in the interest of the country, during the days of the Revolution. In those days he was at the height of his power. Later they did to him exactly what he said he would do. People told on him, and the exact decree that he'd issued here was enacted upon himself.*

You get the feeling that none of these people would've given the same answers a year earlier or later. It was all about that particular moment.

Yes. I believe that this film couldn't have been made, except at that particular time. The conditions helped me make it. As you know, the film was banned immediately. It won the Grand Prize at the first Children's Film Festival after the Revolution, and then was banned forever. The reason is that when the new regime took over, values changed as a result of their power. The decree was that everyone had to spy on everyone else. So, if you wanted to make this film now, I don't think anyone would be willing to speak openly in front of the camera.

People always have two personalities. One is real and the other is like the clothing he puts on when he leaves the house. A government official told me that our problem is that when we speak behind the podium we say one thing, and when we're in private we say something else. The microphone serves only to preserve power. There are two kinds of people: those who speak into the microphone because they have power, and those who don't have power or a podium at all. The common people love to give power to individuals and then keep them there. For this reason,

---

* Sadegh Ghotbzadeh, a close aide of Ayatollah Khomeini before and after the Revolution, was named managing director of National Iranian Radio and Television in February, 1979. He later became the Islamic Republic's Foreign Minister and ran for president in 1980. In 1982, he was executed for allegedly plotting the assassination of Khomeini and the overthrow of the Islamic Republic.

whoever demands power often can get it very quickly. There's a book that I've read in translation called *The Psychology of Power*, and another is by Erich Fromm. They both explain this very well. Fromm's book is called *The Anatomy of Human Destructiveness*. He says that when one's sole desire is to acquire power, one can get it very easily. Some like to get it and some like to give it. It's a very easy deal. I think *Case No. 1, Case No. 2* makes this very clear.

Did you shoot the film's interviews while the American hostages were being held?

No.

It was before then?

The film was already finished. The Nest [of Spies: i.e. the American Embassy] was taken over ten months after the Revolution and the film was finished before that.

There was a romance of student solidarity that may have anticipated the Embassy takeover.

Yes, it's possible.

One detail is the inner ear that the teacher draws on the blackboard and how that resonates with the idea of noise and listening, as in spying.

It was very symbolic. Although I hate symbolism, the ear was the best symbol for the issue. The Persian proverb *Goosh khabandan* refers to a kind of spying. It means that someone expanded their ear in order to hear better. The film begins with this idea. It's about listening to something that isn't your business.

"Toothache"
(26 mins., color, 1980)

Though much of this film is a straightforward lecture about dental hygiene delivered by a dentist facing the camera, it still manages to be persuasively Kiarostami-esque in how it describes young Mohammad-Reza's life at home and school before he falls prey to tooth woes. That some audiences find the film hilarious testifies to the humor that can accompany great discomfort.

Cheshire: *Let's move on to "Toothache." The film is incredibly funny.*

Kiarostami: They showed this film in the Czech Republic last week. You wouldn't believe it, but the audience laughed a lot. I was there myself, and it was the first time that I saw it with an audience. It's a 16mm film.

"Toothache" was shown on television, and the next day there were no toothbrushes or toothpaste left on the market. This isn't an exaggeration. They requested that the film be shown again, and it was shown a week later. Afterward a lot of complaint letters arrived at the TV station. They complained that their children would wake up during the night and say that they hadn't brushed their teeth. The children were all too worried about their teeth. It seems that it had put too much pressure on the children. Although they had brushed, they would wake up and say they hadn't and would brush again.

I made this film because of an experience I had with my sons Bahman and Ahmad. When they were little, they would ask my permission not to brush their teeth at night. I understood this from their point of view, because they didn't know why they

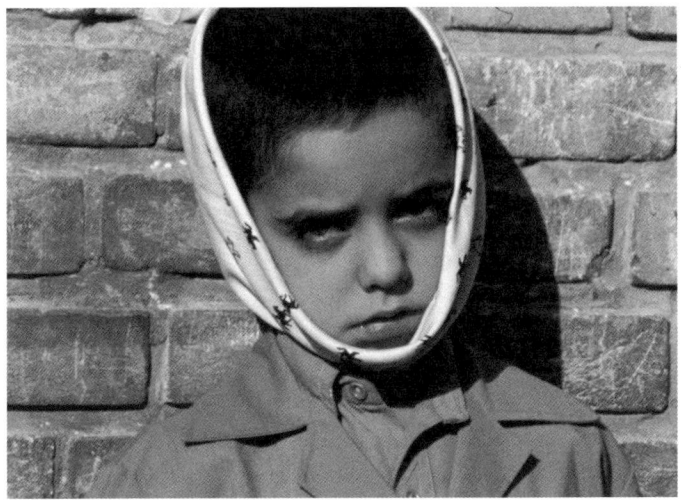

were doing it. They would put some bad tasting thing on something and put it in their mouth. They didn't even look good while doing it. That's why I said that something must explain why they have to do this. So it wouldn't be my responsibility and they wouldn't ask for my permission. They could decide for themselves. In the film I showed that tiny creatures would come with picks and cause toothaches.

Please don't think that I hurt that child's tooth. Many did think I'd hurt him.

That kid did a great job acting, because he looks like he's really in pain.

He was really in pain, but it wasn't my fault. We took the camera to a dental office and found him there, ready to have his tooth pulled out. This is shown in the final scene. We shot it first and then created the rest of the story based off of it. So the film was shot from the end to the beginning. The tooth pulling was filmed as a documentary and then, when his pain was gone, we filmed the rest.

When the dentist is talking to the camera, is the little boy whimpering, or was the sound added later?

No, we shot that separately. We put a man in a white shirt behind him.

There's another extraordinary moment, when the two kids are sitting on either side of the teacher. The first asks the teacher if he can sit on her other side, and she says yes. The second then asks the same question—if he can sit on her other side. She asks why he wants to go to the other side and he says, "Mohammad Reza's breath stinks." This moment is real. The first boy doesn't know that this is in the script—he thinks his breath really smells, and is confused and ashamed. That reaction is so beautiful. For a moment he sits alone and thinks. His reaction shows the shame he feels about his own mouth. This tends to make the audience laugh a lot.

"Orderly or Disorderly"

(17 mins., color, 1981)

The first shot shows students descending a staircase in a calm, orderly fashion, then the second details the same action as a chaotic rush. Separated by slates and Kiarostami's voice intoning, "Sound, camera," subsequent sequences describe the same dichotomous behavior in a schoolyard, on a school bus and looking down on the haphazard traffic of Tehran. Kiarostami described this as "a truly educational film," but it plays more like a quirky philosophic aside.

Cheshire: *The next film is "Orderly or Disorderly," which looks back to "Two Solutions for One Problem" and also looks ahead to* Fellow Citizen, *where you deal with the traffic in Tehran.*

Kiarostami: Yes, even for myself, "Orderly or Disorderly" is a truly educational film. But when you make an educational film, in my opinion, you have to think more cinematically, because some people think that "educational" means only giving advice. In fact, in an educational film you should avoid giving advice, and instead should put a mirror in front of people to show them themselves. I think "Orderly or Disorderly" does this very well. It shows you that, when people do things "regularly," everything gets done better. It may seem as though making an educational film is very simple, but it's very difficult. You must know psychology, sociology, and the relationship between the two very well. You have to know the mentality and particularities of a people. After combining all these things with non-condescending language, you must then put the mirror exactly in front.

"The Chorus"
(17 mins., color, 1982)

An old man strolls through the noisy streets of Rasht and when his hearing aid is knocked out of his ear, the film's sound goes off, mimicking the silence that envelops him. At home, the same thing happens when he takes the device out, and Kiarostami intercuts his silent actions with the clamor of schoolgirls who try to get his attention from outside. Another Kiarostami meditation on the contrasts of silence and sound, age and youth, solitude and solidarity.

Cheshire: *Let's talk about "The Chorus." I believe you told me you don't like it.*

Kiarostami: I don't like it. It seems to me that it's a little too long. It's my only film that seems long to me.

One thing different about it's that you use filters. The light is diffuse.

We added it because of the deafness of the character. Since he, the old man, was deaf, we diffused the surroundings.

My feelings about my own films aren't reliable. Whether I say I like them or dislike them is influenced by the reaction of the first audience to see the film. There have been instances in which I've watched my films with a bad audience. Once I saw two people cough, one person get up and leave, and another one talk to his neighbor, so I thought, *What a boring film* and I left. Then there have been films that I watched with a good audience, and I thought: *What a great film!* Because the audience is paying attention I see that it's a good film. Without an audience a film is dead, it doesn't have an identity—everything is decided by the audience. "The Chorus" was the same.

A film in the can is a film that no eyes see. When people's eyes look at the film on a screen, that's when it's exposed. A film is exposed twice: once when it meets the light and once when it meets the audience's eyes. I've walked out of the theater while watching my own films and never wanted to see them again. I saw part of *And Life Goes On* here in Tehran, where people were noisy and went in and out of the theater and left in a very sad mood. However, I saw it again in Japan because I wanted to check the sound and image quality. I sat in the balcony looking at the audience and they were like stone, with the reflection of light on their faces. They didn't move at all, no one even crossed or uncrossed their legs. I looked at this audience and believed the film was good. So that time I watched the film I liked it very much! I never think about the audience during filming, but afterwards they become my God. They can destroy me and force me to leave the theater. That's why I never go to the theater to see my films. At Cannes during the screening of *Taste of Cherry*

I had my eyes closed. I had to be there so I closed my eyes to avoid seeing someone leave. I also covered my ears.

What memories do you have of "The Chorus"?

Let me tell you about a memory I think is very important. When I told the soundman to record the sound the way I wanted, because this is a film about sound, he objected. He told me to accept that the Revolution had happened, and that the days of ordering the crew around were over. It was they who would decide how to record the sound. That was very strange to me.

Last time I saw "The Chorus" I liked the film's sound very much, and realized that this method of cutting out the sound has existed in me for many years. This is something I did in *Close-Up* as well, when I turned off the sound during the film's last scenes. I did the same in *Homework*.* When you eliminate the sound the image gains more value; and vice versa. It's similar to what happens with blind people: since they can't see their other senses, such as hearing and touch, are stronger. There's an extraordinary potential in cinema for these two things, sound and image, to work with one another in a cooperative and very civilized way, like a duet, like two musical instruments. When one is silent it gives opportunity to the other. In *Homework* the impact of this was outstanding. The silence in the scene when the kids are working is very powerful, and this is something that came from the film itself. If you try to add something from the outside, just for the sake of technique, the film will reject it. Ideas that come from the film itself, on the other hand, protect it and make it better.

---

* *Homework* doesn't have its own section in this book because, during our trip to Koker, I simply forgot to return to it after discussing the Koker Trilogy. The other film not covered, "How to Make Use of Leisure Time: Painting," a Kanoon short from 1977, wasn't a part of Kiarostami's filmography when I interviewed him.

Fellow Citizen
(53 mins., color, 1983)

Kiarostami's fascination with both Tehrani car culture and the uses of power in post-Revolutionary society combine in this documentary about a traffic officer assigned to enforce driving restrictions in central Tehran (a locale near Kiarostami's office at Kanoon). The officer, a rock star in his own world, remains coolly authoritative as he faces a steady stream of exasperated motorists.

Cheshire: *Let's talk about* Fellow Citizen.

Kiarostami: I had Kanoon's projector in my car, so I went to the traffic cop and told him that I needed permission to park there so I could take it into the office. He said this wasn't possible. After I showed him my card he was finally forced to agree. I promised to come back in one hour to meet him. This was at 8:30 in the morning. So I left, and I was busy until one in the afternoon—I'd forgotten about him. When I later passed by the same area I saw from afar that someone else was arguing for a parking spot, just like I had earlier. I realized that the traffic cop had been doing the same job for six or seven hours straight. This had a strong impact on me. The situation I saw was exactly like my own that morning. In fact, it was a mirror image. I saw myself, stood there adding pressure to a man who was already under a lot of pressure. And he was suffering from having to repeatedly say no to people.

The next day when I went to work, I picked up a lot of 16mm film—some of the outdated negative we had. We put the negative in the 16mm camera and went to that same spot and started to shoot. I thought we had to show this to people,

so they would know what a terrible thing they were doing without realizing it. In the rest of the world, when they make a law, they put up a specific sign, saying something such as: "Do not enter." But, here we have a person of flesh, blood, and feelings standing there against five hundred people, from six in the morning until three in the afternoon. And everyone thinks that he himself is an exception. Everyone, instead of seeing the person who works there, only sees his own problem. When this film was done it had the greatest impact on my group, and on myself. I won't argue for a parking spot again. I've never done it again. There's an extraordinary violence in this film, it's horrible. You can easily see a sort of Iranian psychological and sociological behavior. We've always had the habit of condemning the government but, from this film, it's easy to have pity for a government that seeks to govern these people. It's impossible to govern them. I realized why people immediately accept any law: they know they can use the amendments to their advantage. And every single individual thinks that he is, in fact, an exception.

It's hard to govern these people because they know how to zigzag through things. Some moments of the film are truly violent. There's a scene where a man is fighting with the traffic cop, asking him why he doesn't let him have a parking spot, and you can see he wants to beat him. During that scene, while he is shouting, another person says to the traffic cop: "Mister, don't listen to him. I need to go to the doctor." The other angry guy says: "I'm a physician and I need to go to the university to teach. I'm a university professor." The poor cop says: "No, you cannot go in." The angry man replies: "Are you saying that future doctors must not be educated? Are you against medical training? Don't you ever get sick yourself? Don't you need a doctor when you get sick?" The poor traffic cop says: "Yes, they have to be educated. Yes, I also get sick." This scene is terribly violent. It's something like when a gladiator is put in an arena and thrown to the lions. The film has many incredible moments. Sometimes it gives me a lump in my throat.

It's funny and it's very emotional. It also seems that these things happen at the level of their subconscious.

Yes. That's why I say it's very animalistic.

It's also a little bit abstract, in a way. The pattern of these people coming together, where you can forget about the emotional aspect.

The film has a fixed view, with the camera in just one spot. It was all shot from this same angle, with the same tripod height and the same lens. The camera is static, and people enter and exit the frame one by one. The other interesting thing is that we thought we'd have to hide the camera, but we didn't have to because no one would have believed themselves to be the subject of a film. So the camera was left in full view. The people trying to get by were so focused on trying to fool the traffic cop that they didn't even care about the camera. It wasn't important to them, they just wanted to pass through. There was only one man who, when he saw the camera, thought its presence more important than him getting past. He asked us if we were making a film and, when someone in the crew replied that we were, he started to stare into the camera.

This is the only instance in which the common people and intellectuals behave in the same way. There's no difference between their actions. Usually you can easily see the difference between an educated person who wants to cross the street and an illiterate person.

Was the film shown in any festivals?

Nowhere. This one was banned immediately. During the time we were making the film the law of the veil started to be strictly enforced and, in this film, you can see women who are not wearing proper veils. So it was banned. Initially, it was supposed to be shown on TV. What's interesting is that, when we showed the film for the first time, we invited the head of the traffic department, TV officials, ten traffic officers, and traffic experts. When the film was over there was a long silence. The traffic chief came forward and said: "Of course, it was a very good film, but the ladies didn't wear proper hijab." The thing is that hijab had nothing to do with his jurisdiction. And the head of the TV department said: "By the way, some of the people in the film called some of the streets by their old names, names that were used before the Revolution." We'd invited them to see the film and give their expert opinion, but instead they gave opinions on women's hijab and street names. Anyway, like *Homework*, this was a document to show how people easily credit dictatorship.

The film stayed banned?

Within Iran it's banned, but it can be shown outside. They showed it outside Iran. But among my films the following films are banned both in Iran and outside Iran: *Experience*, *A Wedding Suit*, and *Case No. 1, Case No. 2*.

I don't understand why Experience *and* A Wedding Suit *are banned.*

Because the first censor to see them said no, and no one else was willing to watch them. But there's no danger in being banned. If you release it and put it out there, that can be dangerous. There's a proverb that goes: "If you don't write dictation, you don't risk spelling mistakes." The most accurate dictation is the one that isn't written. According to this philosophy many people don't do anything.

So the films that are banned inside and outside of Iran are Experience, A Wedding Suit *and* Case No. 1, Case No. 2. *Is that all?*

Yes. As well as *The Report*.

First Graders
(84 mins., color, 1984)

Inspired by his work at Kanoon and his own sons' schooling, the first of Kiarostami's two documentary features about education looks in on a schoolyard of chanting, playful boys but mainly transpires in the office of a supervisor who has to deal with latecomers and discipline problems. You can almost see the boys' personalities forming in their first encounters with authorities and fellows from outside the home.

Cheshire: *Next was* First Graders.

Kiarostami: I don't want to say that *First Graders* is an important film, but I'd like to say that it's a very important document, because it shows how violence can drastically change children's behavior while they're still in a state of innocence.

And this is much more intense in a country like ours than in other places. One day you wake up and they tell you that you must be responsible, and that you are a man now. In this film it's mentioned several times that "you are a man now, you mustn't cry."

In several instances, these kids are being punished because they've broken promises. But there's a saying in English that goes: "Promises are made to be broken." The adults don't know that a promise is there to be broken. Unless you break your promise, you don't grow up. It's like when a child falls down: they say that unless a kid falls he won't grow up. So, if you don't break your promise, you don't learn.

If you watch *First Graders* once with this point of view, you'll see that it's a very violent film, because the adults in the film expect too much from the children. You can't even expect this much from adults. All of a sudden, the children are thrown into a prison of educational laws.

Where Is the Friend's House?
(83 mins., color, 1987)

The poetic humanism of Kiarostami's child-centered films is epitomized by this, the first of his features to gain international renown. In the village of Koker, a second-grade boy mistakenly takes home the notebook of a pal, then launches on a quest to return it. The shifting power relations between adults and kids, along with Kiarostami's acute visual sense, give the film the fascination of a multi-leveled fable.

Cheshire: *Your first narrative feature after the Revolution was* Where Is the Friend's House?.

Kiarostami: I'd had an inner revolution while we had an external revolution. My inner revolution had taken place during the making of my last narrative feature film, *The Report*. The feature made after my inner revolution was *Where Is the Friend's House?*. The difference between these two features is the difference between me before the inner revolution and me after the inner revolution. That's exactly how it is.

Before Where Is the Friend's House? *you made the documentary* First Graders *and afterwards you made* Homework, *another documentary about school children.*

I think that *Homework*, *First Graders*, and *Where Is the Friend's House?* are all, in reality, one film. Someone—I can't recall who—said: "People only make one film in their life, but divide it into pieces. Every one or two years a new piece is shown." Therefore, one can find traces of *First Graders* in *Where Is the Friend's House?*. And the lead in *Where Is the Friend's House?* is one of the kids in *Homework*. Plus, all the children in *Homework* could be Hossein Sabzian in his childhood.

Let me ask you more about your "inner revolution" and how that affected your work?

The effect of my personal life on my work is much more significant than anything else. The credits for a film should mention the director's moral support during its making. This is more important than the director of photography, cameraman, soundman, editor, or all the others. It's an absent person who's present at every single moment of the work.

How did your own life affect the creation of this film?

The concept of this film comes from something very personal and also from another idea.

Let me briefly tell the personal story, which is about Bahman when he was in second grade. A woman who was a friend of ours came to visit. She'd always been kind to Bahman since he was little. Whenever she came, Bahman would sit in her lap while we talked. But on this visit she'd just lost her job and was very nervous. Bahman was standing there watching us. He was very small, around six. He kept looking at us, wondering why he wasn't on her lap. At one point she asked me if I had a cigarette and I said no. But then Bahman interrupted, saying that we did have cigarettes. I knew Bahman was lying, because we didn't have any in the house. But Bahman said we had some in the refrigerator and went to look. He returned saying we didn't have any, and then went to search the rest of the house, faking it. I knew he just wanted to communicate with her, and this provided him with the excuse to do so. So, when there weren't any, he said: "If you want, I'll go and buy them for you." Then, my other son Ahmad said: "I'll go." He was older but, as I knew Bahman really wanted to do this, I told Bahman to go buy them. So he went. I told Ahmad to run and make sure that Bahman had something on, since it was winter, but Bahman was already gone. After much time, Bahman hadn't returned. We got worried and went out to look for him. Then we realized that it was Friday night [the Muslim holy day], so it was dark and everything was closed. We searched for an hour and a half but couldn't find Bahman. Suddenly, we saw him appear in the darkness with a pack of cigarettes in his hand. We asked him how he'd managed to buy the cigarettes, since everywhere was closed. He said that he'd gone to Ekhtiyarieh, which was surprising since it was four kilometers away. Ekhtiyarieh was close to Bahman's grandmother's house and he knew there would be stores open, since it was a very crowded and popular area. He was wearing only a shirt. I hugged him because his sense of responsibility was extraordinary to me; he knew that he couldn't come back without the cigarettes. Seeing this in Bahman was very emotional for me, something that stayed with me for a long time.

I also heard another similar story that a schoolteacher told me, and I combined this with Bahman's story to come up with the idea for *Where Is the Friend's House?*. The long trip didn't exist in that story: the teacher had only seen that one boy's homework had been written by another boy. Bahman's sense of responsibility was combined with this other story and became my film.

Which of these happened first?

Bahman's story took place first. I've lived with it for a long time. You cannot feel now what I felt that night. You don't know how long the walk was, you don't know how dark it was. It was absolute darkness. That trait has always stayed with Bahman, and he is still like this, even now. If he goes out to get something he won't come back without it.

I want to tell you another story about Bahman. When he started living with me he was five, and we used to live upstairs, right here where we live now. I had a workshop where I did woodwork. That place was full of sawdust. Their mother was gone, the kids were now living with me, and I was on the verge of a mental breakdown from managing this new life. Bahman always kissed me before going to sleep. He hadn't learned this from anyone—it wasn't a habit we had in our home. I was doing some woodworking late one night and the place was full of sawdust. Bahman came in barefoot and said: "Daddy, kiss." He wanted to go to sleep. I saw that he was barefoot and, as I was in a bad mood, I hit him on the back of the head. Instead of kissing him, I hit him and said: "Kid, how many times must I tell you not to come in here barefoot?" His head hit the door and he left crying. You can imagine how much worse I felt then. After a while I heard a woman coming upstairs, which was very confusing—who could it be at this time of night? The house was locked. I heard clack, clack, clack, and then Bahman came in. Not having found his own slippers, he'd put on his mother's old high heel shoes and come back crying for a kiss. He meant: "Even though you hit me, a kiss is still in order." I'll never forget his feeling of propriety.

I've learned so much from Bahman; we were so close. My sons had the bad luck of growing up without their mother, but I had the good fortune to learn from them up close. There are so many stories like this that helped me discover the incredible beauty of my children's point of view; their amazing way of looking at life. There's a saying from a writer—I don't remember the name—that goes something like: "The difference between the human being and the silkworm is that the latter are worms in the beginning but then transform into butterflies, while the human being is born a butterfly and then changes into a worm." When children grow up they change into beasts, which is us now.

What kind of script did you have for Where Is the Friend's House?

I'd written the script for another person to direct. He was a poet named Farhad Sheibani, who was somewhat familiar with filmmaking. But when he changed his mind, I continued writing the script. It was relatively complete; written almost entirely.

When I interviewed Mohammad Beheshti[*] he told me he'd seen the script for Where Is the Friend's House? *and that he urged you to make it even though you wanted someone else to direct.*

---

[*] One of the young Islamist intellectuals who helped revive Iran's cinema after the Revolution, Mohammad Beheshti served during the 1980s as the managing director of the Farabi Cinema Foundation, the organization within the Ministry of Culture and Islamic Guidance that oversees cinema.

Yes, he is right. You wouldn't believe it, but I kept thinking: I wish the [Iran/Iraq] war would come to Tehran so I wouldn't have to make this film. I didn't think I could add anything by directing it, as in my mind it was finished. But I'd signed the contract, everything was ready, and I didn't have any excuse to avoid making it. Beheshti is telling the truth—he really pushed me to make this film.

So you didn't change the script during the making of the film?

That's correct. I don't think that many things changed while we shot it. I made what I'd written.

This story could've been set in Tehran but you chose a more remote location in and around the village of Koker. Why is that?

Since I was making a poetic, heroic work, I thought it would be better to have rich, green spaces. The city lacked this aspect. I was also looking for a place where the children didn't have heavy accents. Unfortunately, in our country there are jokes for all the different regions, so I was looking for a place that didn't have a Tehrani accent and didn't belong to a specific province. I kept looking around with the help of another director, Kambiz Partovi, who made *The Fish* and who comes from that region. We went there and, as the people spoke in the urban fashion with just a hint of an accent, I chose it.

Are all the actors in the film from that area?

Yes, everybody. I found the main child in a crowd at a place called Imamzadeh Hashem. There were one or two hundred men who were struggling to transport a large dome from a truck to place it over a shrine. It was as big as a house. This kid was among other children. I saw in his eyes that he was worried about the fate of this dome—that when they put it down it might fall, break, or be damaged. While the other kids were just playing, he was looking at the scene, from far away, with worried eyes. It was all in his eyes. This was the first thing that attracted my attention. He was useful to me, because for the whole length of the film I needed those worried and troubled eyes—the theme of the film is worry and anxiety. I don't know who said it, but to find a good actor, you just have to look at their eyes—you can see the soul just by looking into the eyes. Not only did he have these eyes, he was also a truly responsible boy. And very sensitive.

So choosing this boy wasn't difficult because we found him right away. The main issue was getting his parents' approval, because his mother was against it. I paid the family well, promised to hire a private tutor, and bought them gifts, but none of these things could gain her approval. There was a very interesting reason for this, which we discovered suddenly. When we went to pick up the child, the mother cried and moaned, saying: "You cannot take my child into the film." Then we found out that she'd seen only one film in her life, many years earlier. It was an Indian movie in which a kid gets lost, and only returns when the mother is old and blind. She thought that if her son acted in the film he would get lost and would come back only when she'd become old and blind. She didn't think that he would come home every night, but thought he was going inside the story. Her mind was fixated on this: the film, the disappearance of the child, the blindness of the mother.

Did you think of using this story in Where Is the Friend's House*?*

Yes usually I would, but this story is too incredible. It's unimaginable. You have to know that I'm smart enough to avoid going after stories that are too incredible. I've enough intelligence.

You used two brothers, Babak and Ahmad Ahmadpour, to play the main boys, who aren't brothers in the story.

Yes. Since there was no resemblance between the two, I could use both of them. We made a deal with the whole family. We also hired the father as part of the crew, as the assistant to the cook. My assistant, Kiamars Poorahmad, wrote a book about the making of this film. If you want to know what the book says in one sentence, I'd say that the making of the film in itself is a totally separate story, a whole other adventure.

This boy, Babak Ahmadpour, really believed that he'd taken another child's notebook by mistake. This is the truth. If the film touches your heart, it's because every moment with that child is real. He never "acts."

So you try to make children believe the fiction of the film is true?

Look, you have no choice; you have to create the right conditions if you want to work with children. You can't just ask a kid to cry and expect him to cry. There's no other way. You have to give him the dialogue, but he has to find the emotion.

One of the reasons why I don't want to make films with children anymore is that I don't want to continue this game. When an adult actor wakes up in the morning, he is under a lot of pressure but, since the adult understands money and fame, he tolerates the pressure. But children don't understand this. Children don't look for fame, therefore they truly get oppressed. But not adults. They sign a contract, but this isn't the case with children.

How did you decide what to show of the villages?

We see the details. The details and the whole. On the one hand, we see the village from afar, from a great distance, so we can understand the location. On the other hand, all the other views are the size of the boy, and deal with the human element in the village. For the most part, the camera has the human view, not the geographical one.

I've never looked as hard for a location as much as I looked for this one. I spent almost a year looking for it. In fact, I visited three villages that were nearly 300 kilometers apart. The Ahmadpours' house is actually 300 kilometers from Koker. It was in Masuleh.

And the hill is outside of Koker?

Yes. That hill is very famous now. People come from Japan to see it—tourists really go there to see the hill, to walk up and down that hill. *Where Is the Friend's House?* is very famous in Japan.

Was the hill already there or did you make it?

I had a mental image of a hill with a tree, which he walks up. I found that tree on the hill, and then we made the path.

So you had a mental image of the hill, and then found it in reality?

That's absolutely correct. It was a dream—just like the image in my mind. The hill has this significance: the zigzag path means hardship, and the tree means friendship.

The theme of a quest is a common one in Iranian literature. Is that what drew you to this story?

It does seem that the theme of a search attracts me; the search is always there. But I don't arrive at this narrative through its significance. The significance is inside the form. I had a good experience when I showed the film and talked about it in a workshop. Whatever it was about a scene, whatever memories, mythology, poetry, or associations the scene brought out—they would all come out one by one. These things are all in the film, but I didn't begin with them.

One thing that's interesting about Where Is the Friend's House? *is that it's so convincing about childhood from an emotional point of view, and the world of children seems very much apart from and antagonistic to the world of adults. Each has its own set of rules.*

I don't think this is limited to the worlds of children and adults. In the world of grownups the same thing exists. I've noticed that, many times, there isn't a true dialogue among people. When there's true dialogue, the discourse can go forward and reach a conclusion. So, for example, in *The Report* there's no true dialogue, not just between the husband and wife, but also between the man and his friends. No one truly communicates with anyone else. Everyone just talks about themselves. You see more of this in the world of adults than in that of children.

What I don't understand is that even though adults aren't too far removed from their childhood, they seemingly don't want to remember it. I believe this is because people are unsatisfied with their childhood years, and so don't want to return to them. That's why children can make adults angry: they remind them of this without intending to. The children are innocent and unaware in their own world. I think adults can understand the world of children, but they reject it.

I think the anger that teachers can direct towards children may be rooted in this. They're in the worst position too, because they can see themselves sitting on those benches. Sometimes they may not even know why, but the environment of the classroom irritates them. It's quite sad in a way, because you have a group of innocent children and a responsible adult. It's sad on both sides.

In the film, the worlds are very distinct. The children's world is defined mainly by this one act of kindness, this boy trying to be kind to his friend, whereas the grownups' world is defined mainly by a series of acts of unthinking cruelty.

This cruelty can come from social circumstances.

I think that was made clear in the scene with the grandfather with the coin and the beating.

Exactly. He thinks that this is a kind of revenge and believes that, when he grows up, he has to inflict exactly the same thing.

In his introduction to the translation of Seyavash,* Dick Davis says a recurrent theme throughout the whole poem is fathers killing their children or being inadvertently responsible for their children's death—fathers being harsh on their sons. I see this as a theme throughout your films also.

Yes. Under the guise of responsibility and discipline.

---

* Ferdowsi, *The Legend of Seyavash*, translated with an introduction and notes by Dick Davis (Penguin Books, 1992). The book is a section of the 11th century poem *The Shahnameh* (*Book of Kings*), Iran's national epic.

The pattern of cruelty and innocence is reversed with the character of the old man, the artisan building the window frames. How did you come to create this character?

He is based on someone I knew myself, and his presence was originally just to push the story forward—someone to take the boy from point A to point B. After I imagined him as a carpenter, I then needed a reason for him to help the boy. The other grown-up characters don't talk to the children so he couldn't be an exception unless we showed the reasons for his being one: he's alone, his brother and his brother's children have left him, and he's searching for a listener. He's talkative, and being talkative is a characteristic of old people who're in search of a pair of free ears. This is how someone who was originally only there to move the story forward became a character.

He also has a dreamlike aspect. He seems to come out of the subconscious, in a way.

This character is hard to judge. You can't really tell whether he's helping the kid or pestering him. You can't judge him too prematurely because he's a bit eccentric. If he'd been a bad man, you'd lose your connection with him quickly, so you want, like the child, to have faith in him, and you want to see whether he can be of any help. In a way, at some point the audience and the old man become one: both the audience and the old man want to help the child. But it takes a long time to realize that he can't be of any help. When we have problems we think that mysterious people or heroes can help us more than an ordinary person.

This character, as you say, has a strange job: his stained-glass windows are strange, and he's a bit more than an ordinary person. It's characteristic of carpenters to be calmer than other people.

He couldn't have been a grocer, a butcher, a blacksmith. Those jobs aren't suitable for an eccentric person. When God wanted to pick a lover for Mary, he picked a carpenter. You may not believe it, but in real life, carpenters have an amazing calmness. I've a workshop up there [*gestures upstairs*] for a good reason: it's my meditation room. It's been more than two years since I've gone to my workshop, as I don't need to meditate. [*Laughs*]

Are there men who make wooden frames and put glass in them like that, or is that something you just made up?

It does exist. This kind of work with its attention to detail is like a kind of worship, since you're working with natural materials.

They remind me of church windows in the West.

Yes, they've that significance. The character's presence is such that you don't lose your faith in him until the very end. He releases the child into the darkness and says: "You go, and I'll keep an eye on you from here." You can see that as both positive and negative. Just like a priest, both positive and negative.

It's ironic though, since the climax of the story is that the boy has to help himself.

Yes.

At the climax of the film you don't show him going to his friend's house; it's all in long shot and it's all very dark.

Here I thought I could show the house he'd been to once before with merely a signifier: a horse he'd seen there in the afternoon and an oscillating lamp. Same shot, but one is during the day and one is at night. It's here that I thought, much like with a crossword puzzle, you can bring in the audience. I believe that about half the audience, though, doesn't get a shot like this, because you haven't completely explained things to them. But the half that understands will explain it to the other half. This creates a good wave in the audience that causes them to ask why he didn't give the notebook back to the person it belonged to, and then you remember that this house is the same house he'd gone to before.

When did you shoot Where Is the Friend's House?

Springtime.

Was it an exceptionally difficult shoot?

It was just as we'd predicted. Although eight reels were destroyed in the lab when we came back to Tehran, we still had time to go back to Koker and reshoot. So we had an extra week of filming. The walls had originally been a cream color, and we'd painted them white for the film, so we had to re-paint them, reshoot, and then paint them their original color again.

Did people think you were crazy?

The first time we didn't have problems with people.

Was it hard to reshoot, since you work in a special way with child actors?

Sort of, because each shot is unique.

One thing you haven't mentioned is the poet Sohrab Sepehri, who wrote the poem "Where Is the Friend's House?." Was he a big influence on you?

There was a time in my life when Sepehri had a lot of influence on me, but after a while his influence lessened. When we started, I didn't have a title for the film, and one day while we were driving on the Karaj Freeway, I suddenly said: "Where Is the Friend's House?." That's when I chose it as the film's title. Some things are in my subconscious, which means they aren't too distant from Sepehri's poems. I was influenced by him only shortly before the making of the film. Now I'm not influenced by him.

What was it about his poems that you liked?

Simple to the mind and complex in the content, something that completely changed for me later. Now I prefer both to be simple.

Do you read a lot of poetry?

I used to, but not so much anymore. I say to Bahman that it's strange that he doesn't read poetry, because when I was his age I read a great deal of poetry. I think I read the most poetry before my thirties. Poetry came to me earlier than literature and novels did.

It seems that in some ways your approach to filmmaking is like poetry. Do you see it as specifically being influenced by it?

Without too much modesty, you won't find an Iranian director who's memorized more poems than myself. But it wouldn't be right to say that I make films because I've memorized poems. Poetry is the core of life. Sometimes you find it more in everyday life than in poetry books.

The meaning of poetry has completely changed for me, because the poems I know by heart aren't the same as the ones I like now. I don't really like the poems I've memorized. When I was in London, a friend from the Consulate said that he was going to visit an Iranian patient who was about to die. He had heart problems. I asked who he was, and he named this poet and I cursed him right then and there. I hate him. When I was 16 or 17, I fell in love with his poems. His book cost 25 tomans back then and was very expensive for me, so I borrowed it from my friend and copied the anthology from start to finish in three nights. When I was done, I knew all the poems by heart. When I became a bit more mature I realized the catastrophe. Because here I am, holding an entire anthology of poems in my head without even liking them. It's much like someone who gets a tattoo and then regrets it. So, when I cursed this man, my friend asked why. I said: "Because I've memorized his poems." And his poems were very pedestrian and crude—about how he was in love with a girl, but the girl's family prevented their union—and he'd written those poems in grief. There he was, imposing his grief on us. Then I realized that these weren't poems but mere bullshit. So then I started reciting the poems for my friend, and he said: "Man, these are really good, why don't you come along?" So we got there, and the poet was in the hospital bed and my friend said to him: "This is one of your ardent fans, and he knows a lot of your poetry by heart." Then my friend asked me to recite some for him. At that time the poet was 70 years old. I started reciting on and on and the poet's eyes began to swell up. Then I realized that I'd memorized all these poems so that one day I could go there and, in that exact situation, let him know that there was someone who knew his poems. I was really happy that this trash was actually of some use that day.

The point of this whole story is to say that I've read many bad poems. They weren't poetry; they were just rhymes. It was very hard in those days to find real poetry. Sentimental poems affected me most because of my age. But, gradually, I moved away from them. I also realized that, even in those banal poems, you could still find some interesting details. For example, in *Through the Olive Trees*, when Hossein, in anger, insults the girl as she's walking up the hill, saying: "I only decided to marry you because you were so miserable and orphaned." All that came from a very vulgar, common, pedestrian poem that I had memorized, and there I found a use for it. The poem goes:

> To hell with it, my friend, I don't want you to love me
> Not having you, I won't cry and moan
> Do you think there's a shortage of beautiful faces in
>   this town?

> From this day, I will choose someone better than you
> If you don't love me, that's not much of a surprise
> A crow never becomes intimate with a canary

The poem is about 100 verses, but in the end it reads: "Pity all that came from a broken heart." These are very common poems, but these common poems are appropriate for popular movies. But now the poems I think about are full of images: for example, one by William Carlos Williams. I've a friend in New York who's a poet and whenever we get together, we read Williams' poems. There are also Marianne Moore's poems, which are full of details. In my opinion these kinds of poetic images are never coupled with stories.

At this stage, I think real poetry is Japanese haiku, because it exists outside of rhyme and doesn't tell a story. It just gives you an image that moves you emotionally. For example, it may say that the moon shines uselessly on a barren desert. This is just full of images, like an image of a lover who has mistakenly wandered into a barren desert. And this is what I think can help cinema the most.

There's a kinship between this kind of poetry and cinema that you don't have with other kinds of poetry. Were there any classical Persian poets you particularly liked?

Those guys are in a completely different category. They've a greater message to convey. Without their knowing it, they've contributed a lot to the cinema. They've separated man from this earthly world and shown us another world that's closer to dreams; thus separating man from the banality of everyday life. More importantly, they talk about the philosophy of life. For example, we can't say that Hafez is just a poet; he's a mystic. He has found a more accurate and wiser meaning than we have for life. There's a poem by Hafez that I recite for my friends whenever they're in trouble. It has helped me a lot too. It reads:

> Just as the fortune of our nights of togetherness has passed
> These days of separation will pass also

This isn't just poetry but wisdom, and its significance stems from the dialectic in which it's written; its logic is in its dialectical nature. I'll also mention Omar Khayyam, who's more popular and more famous than Hafez abroad and around the world, because his language and philosophy are universal, and not dependent on any nationality. Art must address all things and not just be contemporary. Fifty years later what it says must still be relevant. That's why these guys have lasted 1,000 years. Many films lose their relevance after ten years and are inaccessible in other parts of the world. If art doesn't approach poetry, it'll be lost. Poetry is what separates one from the world and picks one up. If you wanted to write in one sentence what the responsibility of art is, it's nothing but separating one from the material world.

Are there Iranian poets of this century that you think are particularly important?

I can't recommend anyone in particular. We've three or four good contemporary poets. For me, Nima Yushij is still the best of them, because he never became popular and no one could imitate him. He was the poet of images; that is, word becomes image in his poetry. In his *Six Memos for the Next Millennium* Italo Calvino says that the best literature, poetry, film, or art is that which is spun around one image. That's why I say before words, it's the image that's the mother of all the arts. Even our imagination begins from an image: we first see ourselves at a location, and then the dialogue comes. Much of Iranian poetry is quite forgettable. As it now stands, there are 24,000 young poets in Iran who write poems and sonnets. I've read some of them, because I've three sisters who write poetry, but there's not one image in their poems. This is why I say they're not poets, they just write poetry.

Once when my grandmother was traveling with us, she was silent and then said: "Look at that tree on top of the hill." I asked the reason, but she couldn't say in words what was so interesting. What she was showing me was poetry.

Was that where the tree in Where Is the Friend's House? *comes from?*

I think so. My grandmother died 20 years ago.

Did you show Where Is the Friend's House? *to the kids from Koker after it came out? What did they think?*

We showed it in a classroom on video, but an old man and other adults showed up and put so much pressure on those two kids that I took them out of the classroom. At around midnight I took the kids home and showed them the film on video. When they were watching the film, it was as if they hadn't been in it themselves. After the first several minutes they and their family members were all laughing. The mother once in a while would say she looked fat. But I'd heard that before, because the mother of Reza, who was in "Bread and Alley," had also said that. I realized it's not that they think they're fat, it's because, when there's a close-up on screen, they look much bigger than in real life.

Did the kids like the film and themselves in it?

Yes.

What about the people in the village?

They were laughing. Usually in times like this they say it's fake, because they understand that the relationships are false. I filmed their reaction as they watched the film.

Bahman filmed Tahereh and Hossein as they watched *Through the Olive Trees* separately. The camera was on their faces and they both had the same reaction. They were both nostalgic. When the movie ended, both Tahereh and Hossein were embarrassed and put their heads down. I don't think even actors who have been in porn films have ever shown the kind of shame that they did.

Close-Up
(100 mins., color, 1990)

A poor man is arrested and put on trial for impersonating prominent filmmaker Mohsen Makhmalbaf to an upper middle-class family in the film that gained Kiarostami international critical acclaim. Blurring the line between documentary and drama, Kiarostami for the first time focuses on filmmakers and filmmaking, while provocatively pondering the relationship between cinema and social justice in post-Revolutionary Iran.

Cheshire: *I'd like to talk about* Close-Up.

Kiarostami: I've made two films that I have opinions on, I don't have opinions on the rest. First is *The Traveler*, because twenty years have passed since it was made. I have distanced myself from the film, and therefore feel I'm a part of its audience and no longer its director. At least, I don't watch it as its director. Among all my films, *The Traveler* moves me deeply. The other film is *Close-Up*. When I saw *Close-Up* after its making, there was already a distance between me and the film, meaning that I was again a part of its audience. And it's very strange that Hossein Sabzian, the protagonist in *Close-Up*, sees himself as a character in *The Traveler*.

Does he say that in the film?

There's a moment in the court scene where he says that he feels like a child, that his love is as strong as the love of the child in *The Traveler*.

What he doesn't say is that he was beaten.

Yes. He wasn't beaten in the film, but he has been beaten in real life. When I talked to him on another occasion, he told me about his life and it was very similar to that of the boy in *The Traveler*. The first time he went to see a film, he didn't leave the theater after it finished. He stayed to watch the film five more times in a row. Suddenly, he realized that it was midnight and he couldn't go home. He hid in the men's restroom and waited until everyone had gone. The following morning, instead of going to school, he was tempted to go back into the theater and watch the film again.

Makhmalbaf gave me his story of how Close-Up *started, what's yours?*

I didn't even know Makhmalbaf had a story about it.

Well, he has a story about everything. [Laughs]

I met Makhmalbaf for the first time in a movie theater, and he said he had a screenplay for me to read. So he came to see me in my office. I kept thinking about how after all the insults he'd directed toward established filmmakers, he now wanted to start a relationship with them—I wasn't completely comfortable. There was a magazine on the table and it had an article in it about someone who tricked a family into believing he was Makhmalbaf. I remember that I didn't really like Makhmalbaf's screenplay, and it's hard for me to talk about a script I don't like, so I talked to him about this article instead. We then went to the local gendarmerie where Sabzian was being held. There we asked the soldiers what the story was and things became a bit clearer. I wanted to meet the family, the Ahankhahs, because I thought this situation had the potential to become a film. So, that night we went to the Ahankhahs's house. We rang the doorbell and they looked at me with suspicion and asked me for my ID card. The young daughter told me they had just gotten rid of a fake Makhmalbaf, and they were not willing to deal with a fake Kiarostami. I didn't have an ID card, so I told them that the real Makhmalbaf was sitting in the car, and if they wanted I could go and get him. I brought him in and they served us tea, and we talked about what had happened until midnight. I was fascinated. Three days later I took a camera to the prison. I still wasn't sure that there would be a movie though. I filmed the first part of the film continuously from behind the glass screen. Then I met with Sabzian who introduced himself as Makhmalbaf and thought, yes, I do want to make this.

For forty days [during the making of the film] I couldn't really sleep, even for a moment. Every night I'd close my eyes, then they'd burn, and I'd have to open them because of the pain. I'd take notes during the night and we'd film during the day. We first shot the trial, and after he was released we filmed the rest.

Did you ever resume talking to Makhmalbaf about his script?

No. I gave it to him that night and told him we'd talk about it later. We never did. At the time that *Close-Up* was being shot Makhmalbaf was in Isfahan overseeing the editing of another film. But the day Sabzian was released from prison—which is shown at the end of *Close-Up*—we asked Makhmalbaf to come and meet him. This was the beginning of Sabzian's freedom, but in the editing process we placed it at the end of the film.

Tell me about the head of the court. What's his name?

He's a judge and a religious figure, as all judges are. I don't know his name. To film inside the courtroom we needed permission and this took a long time. As he says in *Close-Up*, the head of the court didn't mind, he just thought we could find better cases to film. He'd said that line to us before, so I told him to repeat it on camera.

By the time you started shooting, had the trial already started?

We created the trial. In cases like this they don't have trials, they just have quick hearings.

Did the family meet Sabzian in court before they were filmed?

No. We sat them down, and then the police officer brought in Sabzian and sat him down. It was just as you see in the film.

So you filmed the only encounter between them? Would that encounter have happened even if you weren't filming?

Yes.

So, the hearing was arranged for the filming. You were sitting near Sabzian and asking him questions? Isn't that unusual?

Yes, normally it isn't done. But in Iran court isn't as formal.

So the judge and family agreed for you to be part of the trial with two cameras?

Yes. I'd told the Ahankhah family to first act tough but to slowly, at my signal, accept his release. I was the director of the courtroom.

What did the family feel about what you encouraged them to say?

They were mad and didn't want to agree to release him, as you can see from the expressions on their faces. At the end, when they suddenly drop the charges, it's because of my pressure and the judge's. They wanted Sabzian to be locked up.

What was your initial impression of Sabzian, and did it change during the course of filming?

I knew it was a complicated case. The day after his release he went to that same judge and complained about me. The judge told him that he was very ungrateful, saying: "Kiarostami got you off, and now you're complaining about him?" Sabzian was complaining because he couldn't believe he'd been released and was being fed good food—he thought he was being tricked. He was quite difficult throughout the shoot, and constantly treated everything with suspicion. He would change his lines. I had written dialogue for him, even for the courtroom scene. The whole thing was his words, I just put them together as I needed them and created connections by saying, for example, "Finish your sentence like this." Not that he was completely against it, but he did wonder what exactly we were asking him to say. He was suspicious that maybe we'd use those lines against him later.

He seems like an interesting man, because on the one hand he seems to be from a poor, underprivileged background, yet he quotes Tolstoy and is obviously smart.

He's quite creative and very intelligent.

But it's natural intelligence.

Yes, he's self-educated.

It says something about Iranian society, that you have people like that. The second interesting thing is what it says about cinema in society. So what happened to these people after the film?

Both the family and Sabzian were very dissatisfied. They both liked the film but they didn't make up. The family felt that, at the end of the film, Sabzian wasn't punished or disciplined the way he deserved to be. They thought the way he was portrayed made him seem innocent—they really believed he'd wanted to steal their money. I told them that I wasn't there to judge. The court judges, I'm filming it.

But, in a way, you manipulated the legal process.

Yes. But I don't think he really wanted to steal their money. I believe he was closer to how he was portrayed in the film.

I really wish I had time to remake the film and this time, instead of having the family complain about Sabzian, I'd ask him to file a complaint against the family for forcing him to be someone else. I don't believe their fault is less than his.

You saw the film "Close-Up Long Shot"* and said you were very affected by it.

As a film, it did nothing. But it did remind me of how smart Sabzian is. I couldn't sleep for three nights because of all the energy that came from him. The film isn't well made, but an intense energy came from within Sabzian.

Have you seen him or talked to him recently?

Three months ago we were supposed to meet, but that was during the Cannes Film Festival. Then I got involved in a film. But it'll happen one of these days. Every year he calls me three or four times and wants to see me.

Maybe you should make another film about him.

I don't think so.

Where did the idea of playing with the film's sound at the end come from?

It came from the film itself, during the scene when Makhmalbaf and Sabzian take off on the motorcycle together. I had the

---

* Moslem Mansouri and Mahmoud Chokrallahi's documentary *Close-Up Long Shot* (1996) contains extended interviews with Hossein Sabzian that offer more detailed evidence of his mental problems than that glimpsed in Kiarostami's film. The film is included in the Criterion Blu-ray/DVD release of *Close-Up*.

headphones on, and was listening to their conversation in the car behind them. Makhmalbaf knew that we were shooting but Sabzian didn't know. Sabzian was pouring his heart out while embracing Makhmalbaf. He even noticed us filming at one point, but nothing mattered to him—he'd forgotten everything. When Makhmalbaf spoke his first sentence, I quickly realized that the film didn't need it. Firstly, Makhmalbaf said: "Being Makhmalbaf has worn me out." Then he added, "Being Makh…" I cut him off, because the film is about Sabzian—I didn't want to conclude the film with Makhmalbaf's extraordinary energy. Makhmalbaf's energy and personality could've overshadowed the entire film. In the last reel of a film you can't add too exciting an element. When it's ending you can't bring in Marlon Brando, for instance, for the last shot. I really like this part of the film, and the opportunity it provided to play with the sound.

Tell me about the reaction the movie got in Iran.

It wasn't good. Most thought it was a propaganda film about Makhmalbaf. Nobody viewed it correctly. Some said that I really screwed Makhmalbaf over, while others said that I portrayed him quite well. I said to them that the film depicts neither viewpoint: I'm not aggrandizing him, nor am I screwing him over. It's not even about Makhmalbaf but about one individual, and about the daydreams of a man when life becomes hard. It's in praise of daydreaming. It's not even about Sabzian really, since, before the film, he was no one. It's about a human being and his dreams.

It's also about the power of movies.

Yes, but still, that aspect is less emphasized. I didn't want to highlight cinema, other than that aspect of cinema that fulfills our dreams. It's about when life gets hard and the daydreams become more intense. We know everything about our five senses, but we never think about our dreams. There was a time when I thought if I were asked to choose between my eyesight and the ability to dream, I'd choose dreams because, even without your eyes, you can live a better life with the help of your dreams. Without dreams, how can one live? Dreams are like the fan in an automobile engine: when the engine overheats, the fan automatically starts working. If the wire snaps, the car won't go forward. With the help of dreams, we can escape from the worst prisons. Actually only the body can be imprisoned—in dreams you can escape the walls. In dreams you can sleep with anyone you want. Nobody can touch your dreams. In a sense, dreams perfectly embody the concept of freedom, as they free you of all constraints. I think God gave human beings this possibility to apologize for all their limitations. This film is in praise of dreams; it's a beautiful portrayal of a human being who has reached a dead end but still has a hold on his dreams.

The first time I saw Close-Up, *in 1992, the editing was different to how it has been subsequently. Why is this?*

Close-Up was shown at the Munich Film Festival in Germany. I was in the audience, and when the second reel began, I realized it wasn't in the right order. I was going to rush upstairs and fix it, but then realized it was too late for that. So I decided to watch the projectionist's version and realized it was better than my own! Back in Tehran I changed the order of the reels. Good films and bad films are like that: changing the reel order doesn't do much; the good ones stay good, and the bad ones stay bad.

And Life Goes On
(95 mins., color, 1992)

After an earthquake killed 50,000 people in northern Iran in 1990, Kiarostami made a difficult journey there to discover if the kids from *Where Is the Friend's House?* survived. A year later, he fictionalized that quest in this film, using two non-actors to play himself and his son. His first film with life-versus-death as a theme, it movingly observes the aftermath of mass tragedy.

Cheshire: *Let's talk about how* And Life Goes On *started. It obviously started with the earthquake. What do you remember about hearing about that earthquake?*

Kiarostami: It was my birthday. I'm never happy on my birthday, and I never celebrate it. One night we were at a gathering and the host, who had found out it was my birthday, had a cake with candles. This was the first and last time I had a birthday party. On my birthday I usually feel pretty unhappy. I asked my physician about this and he said it's normal and that many people feel this way. That night I went to bed and felt everything around me trembling. The next day at lunch I heard on the news that the epicenter of the earthquake had been the filming location of *Where Is the Friend's House?*. I had to go and see what had happened. My car wasn't working, so I called my friends but couldn't reach anyone. Finally, the next day, I went there in my friend's car along with Kiumars Pourahmad and Bahman. The roads were closed and we couldn't continue after some point, so we returned home. Then the next day we went back, and with a lot of difficulty—it took us 14 hours—we got there. It was hell. There were aid-trucks on both sides of the street and the roads were unrecognizable. Bahman told me later I was crying as we walked. We were there for just an hour or two, but we couldn't find the kids because the village had been completely destroyed. We sang the whole way back and were happy even though we hadn't found anyone. I asked myself why it was that going there, before having seen anything, I felt so bad and upset, but, upon returning, even though I'd observed that level of destruction, I was so happy. The film was in fact my answer to myself.

Three days after the earthquake I went to a film festival in Munich, and they showed *Where Is the Friend's House?* and I watched the film from another perspective. Everything had been destroyed and the film had another meaning for me. At the film festival they asked me where Koker was, and I said that now it was nowhere. Then there was a silence, so I said that it had been destroyed by an earthquake. There was another long, deep silence. I began telling them about the things that had happened to me on the trip to the village—things I had seen that first day. When we left the theater, someone asked me why I didn't just make a film about it. I asked him what film he was talking about, and he said: "The one you just told us about." He said if I were willing to film it he would finance it. But at that moment I wasn't thinking of cinema. When I returned to Iran, I found out that one of the Ahmadpour kids had given a message on the radio saying that they—the children from the film—were alive. At the time those kids were very famous and so journalists had found them—they had become a symbol of the children of Rudbar [area in which the earthquake took place]. As I was no longer worried about them, I thought it wouldn't be a bad idea to make a film. I thought this could be the answer to why I felt much better on our way back.

But at the time that you were singing, you didn't know they were alive yet?

No. We thought they were dead. That's why we were singing. When I thought about it, I realized that I always have that sensation when I return from funerals. I used to feel guilty but, when I asked around, I realized that everyone's like that. It's the discovery that, when faced with death, one appreciates life a lot more. Then I found hundreds more stories. From a distance, on that trip, I was only thinking of catastrophe and death but, when I arrived there, the signs of life were much greater and more visible than those of death. Fifty-thousand people had died, but thousands of trees were still standing. The river and the mountains were as they had been before, and death was just a small dot, like a mole on the face of a living person. It seemed that everyone was trying to wipe away the signs of death. For example, the villagers would bury their kids and, at the same time, they'd wash their rugs and carpets and hang them up to dry. These two things side by side had a very strange effect on me. Even though they had lost their dearest ones, people were still preserving themselves. I think this was where my happiness came from: some had died, but life still went on.

This was a very good experience for me in my fiftieth year because I'd always thought that life ended at fifty. I had looked at the age of fifty from a distance but, when I turned fifty, I found out that even this could hold something good. The age of fifty had seemed like a sunset to me and it was hard to take, but when it's night and you turn on the lights, you see that while it isn't daytime, it's still a good night. What's really hard is this passage from day to night. But when you enter night you see that it has its own positive points, and it may even be a bit more beautiful, because at night one feels more secure. Actually, the best days of my life started at fifty.

When did you decide to make the movie?

I made several other trips and jotted down the things I remembered. Back then, some of the events would have seemed unbelievable if I'd put them in the film. For example, on the third day of the earthquake I saw two teenage girls pouring water on a grave and dancing. When we got there early one morning, it appeared as though two people, a husband and wife who had lost three of their children, were making love—their tent was slightly open and the crew had seen them. I changed that a little and put it in the film. These things stayed in my head and started to take shape. Nothing was written down but I drew a broad outline, and we started shooting a year later.

We reconstructed some of the earthquake scenes. The hard part was making people relive that day. But, on the first day, we immediately saw that their vitality, and the power of the camera, solved that problem. When they first arrived on the scene they were crying, but you could immediately see the happiness behind their tears. The bigger problem was that they weren't willing to wear dirty clothes like the ones they'd been wearing that day. For the filming they wore their best clothes, like what they'd wear for a wedding. Two things had gotten mixed together: life and death. Life was before the camera and much stronger, while death was a reality they were going to be reminded of. That day I realized I couldn't make them wear their dirty clothes. Here the words of the old carpenter from *Where Is the Friend's House?* helped me. He said that he didn't understand what kind of art showed people to be uglier and older than they really were. In *And Life Goes On* he repeats that line. So I took that sentiment and asked them to wear their best clothes. They brought out their nicest things: things they'd pulled out of the rubble and restored and I thought, Why not? We're not portraying reality, we're making a film. If I wanted to reset time, I'd reset it to before the earthquake and tell them to leave town. I can't control reality, I'm only reconstructing it. It reminds me of Godard's saying that life is a poorly-made film, but when you want to make a film of it, make a better one.

During the editing, I'd wake up in the middle of the night and wonder where the film would start, because, for me, even in the seventh reel, the film hadn't started yet. Then, when I screened it at the Fajr Film Festival, the public reaction to it was pretty bad. Those who looked at the film from an artistic perspective said that it didn't have peaks and valleys, that as a story it wasn't dramatic. The regular audience said: "You didn't keep your promise. You were supposed to tell us whether those kids were dead or alive." One of them even said to me on the street: "Mr. Kiarostami, it was very nice of you to take us to the top of the hill and abandon us there." The audience felt that they had been tricked. I explained to them that it wasn't important if the kids were dead or alive. Fifty-thousand people had died, twenty-thousand of them children. So what difference did it make if our two kids were among them or not? I didn't want to make a film about whether they were alive or not. That was a simple piece of information you could get from the radio. What was more important was that life was still going on. You can find out about someone's death from the obituaries.

Usually after I first screen a film, I go home and people call me to tell me what they thought of my film, but with this one, not a single person called. I kept checking my phone thinking that maybe it was broken, but we didn't even get a wrong number that night. The next day one of our friends called Bahman and told him that my film was good. Just one person. So when I got home that day, Bahman greeted me excitedly at the door and said, "Dad, this person called and said your film was very good." Bahman had asked her if she was telling the truth or if she only called for the sake of our friendship.

Within Iran, the film's case was closed, but when it became successful outside Iran and won about ten international prizes, they started screening it again and watching it with better intentions. Even a lot of Iranian critics admitted that they had initially made a mistake. It was a film made on the basis of an inner emotion, and that's why its plot is so simple. The biggest problem for the film was religious people's reaction to it, saying that I'd manipulated people's feelings and ignored mourning ceremonies.

And Life Goes On *has the feeling that it's much less scripted than your other films. Is that true?*

No, *Close-Up* was less scripted than *And Life Goes On*. But, yes, compared to *The Report*, it was merely a line. I was writing the dialogue while shooting and didn't have a full script when we started. The film was produced by Kanoon. I had a very good relationship with the director of Kanoon at the time, Mr. Zarrin. He'd great confidence in me, so I could easily get approval.

That's a real luxury you have, compared to other directors.

Yes, I've been very lucky. Of course, when I talk about using a certain technique, this doesn't mean I reject other ways of doing things. When my students want to work like I do, I don't let them. They must plan in great detail before shooting.

Did you shoot more for And Life Goes On *than you used in the film?*

In general, I shoot much less for my films than other filmmakers. For *Taste of Cherry*, there were only several scenes I wasn't able to include in the film, and that was because the film would've been too long and the quality of the footage wasn't good. But, as a general rule, I've never filmed a scene I didn't use. The reason is that when I get an idea, I don't shoot it immediately. Others approach this whole business too eagerly. They just shoot something without knowing where it's supposed to go or what it's connected to. For this reason, when I get an idea I wait at least 24 to 48 hours to decide how it'll connect with the rest of the film. Then I know what to do with it. Something that's stumbled upon immediately isn't, in my opinion, suitable to be filmed—if I do decide to include it, it needs to be recreated later. The reason this kind of filmmaking uses much fewer negatives is that you only have one or two takes, while in regular films with actors you need as many as seven to eight takes.

So you basically construct the story as you go along and don't shoot things you're not going to use.

Yes.

Did it occur to you to play the main role in And Life Goes On *yourself?*

It did cross my mind. I didn't do it because I believe that if you're going to be in front of the camera, you need a director behind it. That position can't be left empty—things look different from behind the camera than from the set itself. Another problem is that if you're too pleased with your acting performance, then you'll keep the scene in the film even if the other elements in the shot aren't that good.

Did you spend a lot of time trying to cast the main part?

Yes. In road movies like this that have a lot of close-ups, the actors' faces are very important. I think their face is even more important than their acting. I was lucky that neither Farhad Khayratmand [in *And Life Goes On*] nor Homayoun Ershadi [in *Taste of Cherry*] needed to act—both were just there. I'd seen Khayratmand before at some gatherings, so I called him and asked if he'd be interested in acting in my film, and he said it would be a great honor. Then we didn't talk for six months, and one day I called him and said: "We're shooting next week, take time off from work." He said okay and then called me ten minutes later to say that he didn't know how to drive. At first I thought this was a bad joke, because how are you going to make a road movie with someone who doesn't know how to drive? Then I thought, what if he's telling the truth? I'd been thinking about him for six months so I couldn't just replace him. I requested that for the remaining three days before shooting he go and learn how to drive. The first day he sat behind the wheel on location the camera was in a tollbooth. I hadn't told the crew that he didn't know how to drive. He was supposed to go to the tollbooth and ask if the road was open or not. We had to do three takes because he either stopped a little behind or a little ahead of the designated point. Finally we put the car in neutral and some of us pushed the car slowly—we put a stick at the right stopping point. After the first shot was done I told the crew he couldn't drive. They said that I was crazy, that it would be impossible to continue this way.

In the second shot he was supposed to ask a police officer if the road was open or not, but he ended up hitting a bus. It was a strange day. The camera that was fixed a little ahead of the car was worth 20 million tomans and I, sitting under it, was worth something too, but there was nothing we could do, so he sat behind the wheel and we carried on. Telling you this is to make a point: his not knowing how to drive really helped the film. When he's told in interviews how well he acted, he says, "I wasn't paying attention to my acting at all. I was just focusing on the clutch and brakes. They'd told me that the camera was very expensive, so I was just trying not to cause an accident." In the film he seems like he's worried about the kids—this "weakness" helped the film.

What does Farhad Khayratmand do?

He has a Ph.D. in economics. He's an economist.

Did you think of putting Bahman in the role of the kid?

No. Bahman really didn't want to act. The child's dialogue is mostly Bahman's though. For the first draft I'd put my tape recorder in the car and then Bahman and I would talk to each other, acting out the father/son roles. He helped with the dialogue for *Where Is the Friend's House?* in this same manner too.

The child in the film is the son of Homayoun Payvar, the cinematographer. At the time Payvar wasn't married and was living with his child. I asked him if he could work out-of-town for a while and he agreed, but he asked what he could do with his kid. I proposed that he bring his kid along, and then thought I should create a role for him.

When did you decide on the ending of the film and also on ending with the soccer game?

I already knew from the start that the film would end this way. I knew for sure I didn't want to show the kids because, if I did, the focus of the film would shift. It would become a Bollywood film with a happy ending. Just as in *Where Is the Friend's House?*, where he didn't find the house but found friendship, in this film he didn't reach the kids, but he reached life.

The soccer game is something else. It was a joke by one of the guys in the lab who said: "Kiarostami always has a scene of someone kicking a soccer ball," and I realized he was right. In all my films, unintentionally, soccer has a presence. It started from the first scene in "Bread and Alley" when the kids are kicking the ball, and this is repeated in all my films. Even in *Close-Up* they kick the spray can, and in my last film there's a long shot of a bunch of people getting ready to play a game. Then I discovered that soccer has a wide range of meanings; it's a sport that's different from all the others. It's the cheapest sport in the world, meaning that 22 people can play with just

one ball, and it has the most spectators. It's the only sport you can find in every country. So it's a reflection of life. It also has a beautiful emphasis, which is cooperation—something you don't see in any other sport. In the arts you also see it in orchestra musicians.

You told me about the bad reaction And Life Goes On *got at the Fajr Festival. What did you think of that and also, do you re-edit if you get a bad reaction at the first showing?*

Over the years I've only made two films that have been received poorly. The first was "Breaktime" and the other is this. It's not something you can fix with editing—you can't really play around with its structure.

How do you look at the editing process in general?

I generally edit in my head, so any other editing is mostly technical. The creative process in editing is in the sound. I think you can change a bad film to a mediocre film and a mediocre film to a good one with good sound. In terms of emotions, with sound you can shorten a scene without cutting it. By using sound, you can direct the audience in how to see your movie. Also, with sound you can insert meanings that go beyond reality.

Was there a point in your career where you realized the importance of sound?

It began with the film *Experience*. That was the only film I post-synchronized, because I didn't have on-stage sound recording.

So you worked with the sound afterwards to make the emotions clearer?

The actors struggled to convey the same feeling they had on set during dubbing. In a closed room you can't speak the same way you can in an open space.

Sound is crucial. To make this point, I joke with the people in my crew by saying, "today we have to do sound recording, but bring along a camera to do some filming as well." Sound is the creative part of editing. In *Close-Up*, when Sabzian signed Makhmalbaf's book as his own, it was an important moment in the film, so I added a police car's siren in the background.

Do you think its significance comes from working on a subliminal level?

Exactly. In that scene when Sabzian signs the book, he's the one who determines the length of the shot. His signature was prolonged and created a lull, but I found I could shorten the scene with sound, in addition to adding meaning through my choice of sound. This doesn't mean that the scene actually becomes shorter. It just seems that way, because when the siren comes from a distance and gets closer to the camera, it holds the attention of the audience. Whenever there's a problem, I solve it using sound. Especially problems that arise from the weakness of the work. Sound can make it stronger than it really is. Pierre-Auguste Renoir, the painter said something like: "If, while painting, you make a stain on the canvas, don't throw it out, but see what suggestions it makes to you." Turn a weakness into a strength. That's what sound does.

What about music?

I came to music through experience. I wanted a score composed for *The Traveler*, so a ten-minute piece was composed, but I used only seven minutes of it. Not because it was bad, but because I thought the film didn't really need all of it. Ever since then I've used music even less. Usually just at the ending, as a reminder to the audience that the film is finishing. In general, I feel that many films don't really need music. People often use music to cover up weaknesses in their work. Someone once said that if a film has a director it doesn't need a composer.

How did you decide to use classical music in And Life Goes On?

I was looking for music written for wind instruments, since the film was filmed in an open space and both the atmosphere and the people were wild. In our country wind instruments are used at both funerals and weddings. I came across a horn piece by Vivaldi. The horn wasn't used in chambers but rather for hunting, so I figured it could be effective. For example, piano wouldn't have been suitable for the film. It seemed like Vivaldi had composed the piece for this film! I did the same thing in *Through the Olive Trees*. That clarinet was similar to Hossein's character. You can see him with a clarinet, but not with a violin.

Music is so strong that it can influence an audience all by itself, so if I don't use it, it's because I'm scared of its power. It can impose presumptions and force emotion on the audience. I don't think one should pressure the audience or make them sentimental—I try not to do this even with my images. If I use classical music, it's because I think it doesn't have a nationality. Both Iranian and foreign critics have criticized me for using classical music. I tell them that if they want to keep this music in their possession, and ban others from using it, it'll have dangerous consequences. To extend their argument, you could say: "Leave this territory, it's mine." One of the reasons why I love New York City so much is that on its sidewalks I see so many nationalities and not that many Americans. I think this kind of open-mindedness is a necessity for art. Art's responsibility is to pass over borders. Barbed wire only exists on the ground, not in the sky—you can't draw borders in the sky. Music is like the sky, it's like air. So I think that if I listen to classical music, I also have the right to use it. If we could call the spirits of these composers I think they'd say that their music doesn't belong to any one nation. I saw a concert in Paris that was a fusion of Arabic and Western music, and the audience was also mixed. I felt that the music was bringing them closer together.

Through the Olive Trees
(103 mins., color, 1994)

The third film in Kiarostami's Koker Trilogy fictionalizes the making of *And Life Goes On*. While shooting a scene in that film, the director observes the tension between two actors playing a young man and woman who lost relatives in the earthquake. Probing that dissension lets Kiarostami ponder social inequities that have survived both a revolution and a natural disaster.

Cheshire: *Let's turn to* Through the Olive Trees. *When did you decide to make this film?*

Kiarostami: After *And Life Goes On* I didn't think I'd ever return to Koker, just as I didn't think I'd return after *Where Is the Friend's House?*. Everything was accidental. I saw a behind the scenes photo from *And Life Goes On* printed in *Film* magazine, in which I was talking to the woman who played opposite Hossein. I don't talk much with my actors, so I was curious what we were saying to each other. Then I remembered it was because the woman didn't want to act with Hossein. Hossein wasn't married at the time, and their meeting and interaction was just as you see in *Through the Olive Trees*. Hossein was initially the tea boy on the set of *And Life Goes On* but, when an actor couldn't play the part, we had him do it. While I was thinking about the interaction between these two, I remembered that the first time I went to Koker I looked at everything as a tourist: I felt that class difference was merely an urban problem and that the villagers were all nice to each other. And yet it was class difference that made this woman not want to marry Hossein. Of course city values also exist in the village, just on a different scale. I realized the earthquake could have an additional meaning, and that I could explore these ideas in another film. For example: Hossein says that the woman doesn't want to marry him because he doesn't have a house, but then points out that, due to the earthquake, no one has a house and so now he is equal to everyone else. The earthquake is like an apocalypse or a revolution: it has equalized everyone. You then see this hasn't really happened though. The grandmother says to Hossein: "Are you blind? Don't you see the steel beams going up and that everything will go back to normal?" In reality, no earthquake, and no revolution, can really destroy the values of a society.

Was your frustration with the reception of And Life Goes On *a factor in you returning to Koker?*

No. I think each film is like a birth. No one can interfere with it. *And Life Goes On* was made then and belongs to its own period. I really hadn't taken the audience's opinion into much consideration.

Do you think you alternate between films that keep the audience in mind and those that don't?

I just never think of the audience. Only when the film is complete do I start worrying about the audience. By then there's nothing I can do, so I just hope they like it.

Did you make Through the Olive Trees *because you wanted to say something about filmmaking, or did your encounter with Hossein during* And Life Goes On *become the core of the other film?*

The latter. If anything, I was trying to avoid the "film within a film" idea, but I couldn't think of any other way to make it. When it was over I was happy with the result, but I'd have preferred to have made it another way.

Was it part of your intention to discuss social issues indirectly within a fictional frame?

As I said before, I've no desire to discuss social issues directly because I feel that, once these social realities change, I'm going to have to throw out my film—two generations later they won't understand. So I think that through one character, one human being, I can reach certain truths. I always say I'm only allowed to talk about human beings, and human beings aren't separate from social realities. That's why I said before that when filming in the Metro I had to show its effect on people and not just its construction.

Were people really living in the village during the shooting of Through the Olive Trees, *or was that just for the film?*

No, I asked them to come. By then they had already left.

In Through the Olive Trees, *the woman is silent and only the man speaks. Was this part of your playing with sound?*

This was part of the character development. Because when we say that this woman is ambiguous and is silent, it's better to never see her lips moving, and this ambiguity must come through even in long shots. So, her not talking in *Through the Olive Trees* was much better than her merely saying no, and this helps the character's credibility.

But it's also symbolic of Iranian women's lack of public voice and their under-representation in post-Revolutionary cinema.

I don't think so, and I don't say this because I'm scared of telling the truth. I believe silence is more powerful than words. In real life, I recognize women's leadership capabilities more through their silence. I don't think much has changed for women in post-Revolutionary Iran. I think that if they're under pressure they gain more strength to resist and fight back. Personally, I'm scared of silence. When someone talks to me, at least I know what's going on. Silence for me is like darkness, and I'm more afraid of darkness. I believe the women in Iran are very powerful, and that's why I get annoyed by women who portray themselves as weak.

Going back to the film, from this perspective, the three women in *Through the Olive Trees* are very strong, strong in their silence. The old woman is strong and speaks her mind. Ms. Shiva, who's come from the city, is strong, and Tahereh is strong in her silence as she stands by what she wants. As a 57-year-old observer of women and a citizen of this country, I can say definitely that Iranian women aren't weak. They're strong.

Do you think you'll ever make a film with a woman in the lead part?

Sure. Of course. If in Iran women aren't in front of my camera, it's for several reasons. First, I don't like showing women to be weak or incapable, only playing the role of the mother who just raises a child. Men aren't asked to play just a father. I also don't want to show them as only being lovers to men, and don't like shrews or revenge-taking women. So, these obstacles give me very limited options. Then there's another kind of woman I really don't want to show, and that's the exceptional, out-of-this-world woman: women who are products of man's imagination and don't align with reality. This isn't the case just in Iran. Many films are made in which women have mere decorative roles. It's rare to see a woman as a human in a film. This is my ideal.

I thought, when I was interviewing you in 1994 about Through the Olive Trees, *you were thinking of having the fourth film of this series through the eyes of Tahereh.*

You're right. Sometimes I do think about it. But if I don't come back to the idea it's because making movies is becoming pretty hard in villages.

Why?

Because the villagers were convinced by some newspapers that we portrayed them as stupid. The religious people did that. They wrote that these are people of feeling that I'd portrayed as emotionless.

I don't understand that.

In *And Life Goes On* I portrayed life as it was, but the villagers wanted themselves portrayed as emotional, crying 24 hours a day. They brought their tissues to the movie theater ready to cry but, when they ended up laughing instead, they blamed it all on me. Our villagers are sentimental creatures, full of emotion. So these people became upset, realizing that it wasn't possible to change their representation in the film. But, yes, I've wanted to make that film from a woman's perspective.

I think it would be hard to make a fourth film after the three that you've done, but I think that would be a very good idea. It would add something that wasn't there before.

Absolutely. You'd be looking at it from a woman's point of view.

I want to ask you about the end of Through the Olive Trees. *You have the director of the film-within-the-film in the final scene. So unlike in* And Life Goes On, *where the viewer is implied, in this film it's almost as if the director is directing what is being seen here;*

it's his fantasy. I think it's very ambiguous and different from what you've done before.

Sure. It could be that what has happened is in the director's imagination. So, actually, it could simply be the director's wish that she'd said yes to him. Obviously if he hadn't been touched by this topic, he wouldn't have pursued it. If we ask where the root of this is, it's this: The girl said no to the boy in real life. I mean a generic girl said no to a generic boy. Even if it hadn't happened in real life, the possibility still exists. In my opinion, reality isn't that which has definitely happened, but that which has the possibility of happening. At any moment in time, a girl like her could be saying no to a boy like him.

Do you mind these three films being referred to as the Koker trilogy?

No, if you look at it from the point of view of the location and the story. But, from a conceptual point of view, we could put aside *Where Is the Friend's House?* and add *Taste of Cherry* to the other two and call that a trilogy. Because they're about life and death. I hadn't thought of this before, but the content of *Taste of Cherry* is much closer to that of the other two in that all three are in praise of life and confront death.

Just looking at the Koker trilogy, it has a certain synergy, and the more you see them the more each film seems better because of its connection to the other two. I think it's the arrangement of the three that makes the whole seem greater than the sum of the parts, and it's destined to become more so. What do you think of that?

That's why I say that, when you see all three together, it's more than just film: the Koker trilogy becomes a historical document.

The films are a testimony to each other. For example, in the third film of the trilogy we see the teacher from the first one still going to school to teach. It's a document of the children's growing up, and we come to believe that many homes that were full of life no longer exist. It brings to mind Baudelaire's words, that God is in the details. It becomes like the poetry of William Carlos Williams, because he gives so much detail that you no longer see just the flower but the greatness of nature and creation. In his poetry, a flower isn't just a flower, but so much more. These films are testimonies to each other, and that's why they have such an impact on the audience.

Ezra Pound would point to Chinese ideograms saying that there's one for trees, and one for sun, but put together it symbolizes East. So, if you put two details together you get an idea that comes from the relationship between the two. I think this is true for these films.

Let me add something, too. There's a Persian poem that reads: "Did you not know that the truth of the flower is the sun" and another poem that is now a proverb that reads: "The truth of the sun is the sun itself." Put together: when we refer to something smaller than the sun, we use the flower as a signifier of the sun. But, when we want to refer to the sun itself, there's nothing bigger than it so it becomes its own signifier.

Taste of Cherry
(95 mins., color, 1997)

The first Iranian film to win the Palme d'Or at Cannes, this austere drama follows a middle-class Tehrani man as he drives around the city trying to find someone who will agree to dispose of his body after he commits suicide. Extended conversations with three passengers (soldier, seminarian, taxidermist) elicit different views of life, death and individual choice.

Cheshire: Taste of Cherry *is very different from everything you've done before, and yet also has similarities. So what was the personal impetus for making the film? It's been reported that writings by the philosopher Emil Cioran were an inspiration.*

Kiarostami: I read a book by Cioran. I can't say it gave me the idea, just that it reinforced what was already in my head. The idea had been in my head for many years. I've always thought about whether one has the right to kill oneself. Maybe the root of this lies with my father: he was in an accident and was in intense pain for four years; for four years he slept sitting up. He'd always recite this bitter poem: "I am ready for death/Why doesn't the angel of death come to me/My bad luck is that even death has to be cajoled." That has always been on my mind: if someone doesn't want to live, why should they?

Last night, a friend of mine faxed me something that he'd taken from a book. It was actually an Epicurean philosophy that says we must accept this golden rule: one must suffer in order to appreciate what is enjoyable in life. In sum, as Buddha said, the world is a place for pain. If you don't have a tolerance for suffering—and here I think God has given you a choice—then you can just go. He gives you the option to go. Thus, I think suicide is an option for humans. When you have this trump card up your sleeve, you can live better. Just like me right now driving: whenever I feel sleepy I can just pull to the side of the road and rest. But if I didn't have this opportunity, I wouldn't be able to continue driving. Knowing that I can stop the car, however, I can keep on driving to Tehran. The possibility of suicide makes you responsible for your own life—life isn't imposed on you. If you don't want it, you can "get off." I see it as an existential question. I had all this in my mind and then something grabbed my eye in Cioran, and I thought: That's what I've been thinking all along. Two things give human beings freedom: one is suicide and the second is masturbation.

How are they related?

They both free you from something.

Does this thinking about suicide come from something recent in your life?

I don't want to talk about it. But I do think of it as something positive, and I'm not afraid of the future. When people tell me I should think about old age, that there won't be anyone to take care of me when I'm old and blind, I reply that I don't need anyone. More importantly, I think that as long as I'm creative I'll be able to enjoy living. There are two kinds of suicide: one to avoid responsibility and the other to accept responsibility. For example, when Arthur Koestler killed himself, he'd lived all his life shouldering his responsibilities. Or Jerzy Kosiński, who killed himself because he said he was no longer useful and wanted to exercise his own natural right. If you look at this in a positive light—him saying he's no longer useful—this is a message to all living people: If you want to enjoy life, you must be useful. Even in their suicide some people can give a positive message to mankind. This is something valuable. But most important to me is the concept of freedom in suicide. I was brought into this world without my consent, without having chosen my nationality, the color of my skin, or my parents. Nothing was of my choosing, but whenever I want to leave this world I can.

Your point of view on that, though, is very much at odds with the Islamic/official view. That creates a problem right there. Was that on purpose?

I don't think religion always has a function. If it always did, then in religious countries we'd never have suicide. When suicide happens it shows that religion isn't functioning properly. Here I think art can come to religion's help, that through art we can reach a better religion. That means recognizing that I was born into this world with a purpose, and that I must live responsibly. If I can't do that, then I've a right to not be a burden on the world—this kind of suicide is obviously accepting responsibility. Anyway, if a handful of people want to die, let them. This is the final message of the film: Nothing will happen. If you want to leave this world, to hell with you. Actually, the end of the film takes place six months after the rest of the film. Six months later we go to the place where the character committed suicide and see that, even though he'd died, nothing had really changed. The trees were still full of flowers and nature was alive. He was the only one who had been forgotten. And so, if you're not there, too bad for you, because you're the loser. This is why I say the film doesn't have a negative message.

Taste of Cherry *has more dialogue and seems more scripted than the other features that came after* The Report. *Would you agree?*

Yes, because of the sensitivity of the topic. But I split up the dialogue so that there would be sections full of dialogue and sections of silence. Thus, between dialogues there are needed silences. At the same time, I thought I could save the film from possibly being banned by putting the religious arguments against suicide into the film. Any argument people might want to make about suicide a character in the film already says, so they can't say anything more. It's also a response to the audience's dogma. Sometimes the dialogue seems rather intense. Whenever one of the characters gets out of the car there's a rather long break. So at first there's silence, then the dialogue with the soldier, then silence, then the seminary student gets in the car, then there's silence, then the old man who embodies the philosophy of the film itself gets in, and he's the one who says there's really no

pressure: if you don't want to live, go. Then there's silence. This, I agree with you, is highly calculated, and thus the dialogue was inevitably scripted.

It seems to me that it's possible to say the movie has two messages: one is about suicide, and the other is that art leads to a higher religion. In the dramatic situation of the film, there are two things that are curious. One is that we're not told anything about why the man would want to commit suicide, and second is the need he feels to involve someone else in his suicide. What would you say the reasons are for this?

I didn't give the reason for this because the minute you do, all other reasons are destroyed. The truth is the reason isn't that important. The important thing was that, at some point, he just didn't feel like carrying on. Anyone sitting in the movie theater at that moment can think of their own reasons.

I think the question of the movie is really why you keep on living, why you don't want to die. That's probably why the reason for his wanting to commit suicide wasn't important.

Exactly. The film takes life's side and not death's. [At the end of the film] we see life after exactly one minute of darkness, that's the exact moment we don't show the main character's death and don't tell the audience whether the guy died or not. It was important that life emanated from the screen after that. Then the lights go out and everything is dark.

There's also the question of why he wants to include other people.

What's interesting is when he drives his car into the ditch, all those workers run over to help him. But, before going into the ditch, nobody was willing to help him. People show their opinions by remaining silent. The soldier that ran away, the seminary student who invited him to a meal, and the old man who was willing to help him—all of them are intensely on the side of life.

Right, all three people have different perspectives on life.

Yes. This despite their hardships. See, all those who were drawn into this were busy working. They were doing something.

The most interesting one was the old man. Tell me more about him.

The final old man could be a product of the imagination. He represents existential life. When he's asked if he killed the birds he says yes, but for his work—for life. He's the only one who doesn't put pressure on Mr. Badii. He stands up to Mr. Badii with great strength. Throughout the film he simply imposes his force, which is the force of life, on Mr. Badii causing him to become silent. It's clear that he has dominated the other. You see this even in his tone of voice. Then there's his levelheaded response, given in such a way that it frightens Mr. Badii. Even though it appears that the old man has financial problems and has a sick child, he accepts this job to bury Mr. Badii because he wants to save a life. This shows that he's pro-life. He says: "I will use the money from your death to save someone else's life." So in this one sentence, he provides a lesson on life. But there's still ambiguity in his character. We're not sure if we approve of his aiding Mr. Badii or not. This is what separates him from being either a bad or a good man. He's like the carpenter in *Where's the Friend's House?*.

There are two things about him: He recognizes that death exists but gives Badii the final choice, and he also gives the best reason for living, which is the taste of cherry.

Yes. This is exactly what a therapist or a physician does. He says that in order to get better you need to take this medicine every day. But he doesn't pressure you to do it.

You said earlier that he represents philosophy.

Yes, but for it to not seem like philosophy I put it in the mouth of a less educated Azeri.

But he's sort of a natural philosopher.

Yes, because I think the nature of philosophy is very simple. We have to simplify our words. The seminary student just tells Badii to do this or that based on religion. This is where philosophy comes to life's aid. If you don't believe in religion's dominance it loses its purpose. But, even here, God doesn't abandon someone who's let go of religion, but rather gives him philosophy. That's exactly what happened between the 9th and 12th century, also in the West. The church lost its power and philosophy started taking shape. People found stronger reasons for living. They believed that man himself is God, and that through his own reasoning he can distinguish between good and bad. As a result, religion lost its strength, but humankind gained respect and became the product of a kind of spirituality. Those who reject the religious man's "if you do this without a second thought you'll find salvation" school of thought become absorbed in another way of thinking, and that's philosophy. Thus, in the film, Mr. Badii failed the seminary student's course. That's where the simple old man of the people became his teacher and supported him.

The movie is very philosophical and yet grounded in a very practical matter: suicide.

Someone once said: "I accept that life is shit but there's nothing better." Somehow this became the philosophy of the film. That's what the old man is saying: "I also decided to end my life, but berries are also sweet."

Each of the characters he meets comes from different parts of the country. The soldier is from Afghanistan?

Kurdistan, and the seminary student is from Afghanistan. I had in mind from the beginning that it would be much better if he wasn't Iranian. I wanted the soldier to have some kind of accent to show that he was a stranger, but to also be from a city people hadn't made jokes about, because for most cities people have made jokes. Also, Kurdistan was greatly hurt by the war. He wasn't really a soldier, but on the first day of filming he was one of those people who came up to the car and asked if I wanted a worker. He came in the rush to help the crew. I said, sure, come along. So I dressed him in those clothes and shaved his head.

You never see Mr. Badii and the soldier together, because throughout the filming they never met. In the scenes with the soldier, I'm the one sitting in the driver's seat. He was talking to me. Same with the old man and the seminary student. You never see Badii in the same shot as the other characters. If the soldier sees the film he's going to be surprised, because he's going to think: that wasn't the guy driving, it was someone else. But when Homayoun Ershadi [Mr. Badii] was doing his scenes, I was sitting on the passenger side. It was impossible to do it any other way as there was nowhere else from where I could control the scenes. The best place for me was in the seat next to the actors.

So you never have two-shots of the characters? I find that very interesting because it has a subliminal effect—if you never show the same people in the same frame it puts the viewer in a different place in his own mind, thinking about what's going on with these characters.

Wait, there's a long shot where the seminary student is getting out of the car and the car is going around the bend. That's the one time that two of the actors were seen together.

The Wind Will Carry Us
(118 mins., color, 1999)

A TV crew from Tehran arrives in a remote Kurdish village to film an unusual funeral ceremony but are stymied when an old woman clings to life. Like a fable about professional and personal frustration, this droll drama is the most tantalizingly opaque and allusive of Kiarostami's films, containing numerous references to poetry and several characters who are never seen.

Cheshire: *Where did the idea for* The Wind Will Carry Us *come from?*

Kiarostami: The idea came from someone called Mahmoud Aydin. He had two pages of a screenplay, of which only two lines stayed with me.

Who is Aydin?

He's an idea man who's just started his work as a writer, but none of his screenplays have been turned into a film yet. He's not really even a writer, but an idea man.

What did you like about this idea? What about it appealed to you?

It appealed to me because, most importantly, it had the concept of travel in it: a group of people go somewhere. It was also about death and confronting life. I can't say anything more about what fascinated me, but four years ago I got this idea.

When did you first go and take a look at the village?

Two years ago I found the village. It's a village that, along with its inhabitants, is separated from the world. They don't have any contact with the outside world. They only work hard.

What did you like about the place? Did the place make up your mind to make the film?

I had this idea previously, but the strangeness of the architecture—because it's on a mountain—and the strangeness of the people made it difficult to build a connection with them. Villages that have had tourists know this kind of communication, but these people didn't know anything. For example, even when I wanted to take their picture, I realized that they didn't pose for the camera. No tourists, no one had ever gone there. And no cinema. They had television, but their lifestyle didn't allow for anything new. They hadn't seen strangers.

You feel that their culture hasn't been affected by television.

In my opinion, no. What was interesting for me was that television had been unable to change them, because what separated them completely from others was the amazing amount of work they did in a day. We couldn't convince them to work with us at all, even for a day. The man in the coffeehouse said that he would only go with us for an hour but not longer, because he had to work. So we were forced to use someone else for the rest of the scenes.

The people that visit the village are a TV crew.

Yes. But only after an hour is it clear why they're there. When the main character talks to his colleagues, they say to him that they still don't know what they're doing there or how long they're supposed to stay there. He says that it's always been clear what they're doing there. They've gathered there to do a report on a death ceremony. My style of storytelling is to make the viewer curious, and then give the information in bits and pieces. The only way I can carry the viewer with me is through curiosity.

The ceremony is unusual and only happens in this place?

Yes.

Is this a real ceremony or is it something fictional?

It's a real ceremony based on the real people involved in the ceremony.

Is it Kurdish or is it Iranian?

It's Kurdish and from Luristan. It involves scarring the face during the mourning ceremony. The teacher says that there are two scars on his mother's face.

Is this Islamic?

I think it has roots in Islam, but I don't know from where. But our historical roots are in Islam.

It reminds me of flagellation for Imam Hossein.

Yes, everywhere has their own Hossein. But the teacher gives a very good explanation for the root of it. He says it has economic roots. But it also has another root: When misery-stricken people cry with one another, they create bonds. This brings them closer together, and they become an immense destructive force. They're a force that protests and has a tendency toward protest.

But the economic explanation to me sounds like a modern explanation, while the phenomenon is an ancient one.

Even so, we still end up with an economic explanation: where did this desire come from, this getting together? In my opinion, any time a group of people gets together, at the root there's an economic explanation.

Is there a conscious connection between your film, when they say they're going in search of treasures, and The Secrets of the Treasure of the Jinn Valley *(1974) by Ebrahim Golestan?*

I didn't think of it, but the landscape was reminiscent of Golestan's film. When you find yourself in nature, the roads truly disturb you and transform you. The bends in the road somehow invite humans to go further and distance themselves from one another. The root of this lies in a kind of historical insecurity, because they want to go somewhere where no one else can reach them. These lines are beautiful to me and have a psychological dimension. They haven't been drawn by the state, and so they're truly of the people. This even goes for the houses: when you build houses beside a mountain, you're looking for some kind of security—you want to be in the safety of the mountain.

But the idea of lost treasure is a fairytale idea in a way and is very appealing.

Yes, of course. The idea of lost treasure comes from very poor people, because these people held on to this story so strongly. The best possible way for me to communicate with them was to talk about treasure. It's the only dream that distances them from their misery. Let me tell you a very nice story. Once I saw a graveyard from my car and said: "We're going to dig a ditch here." I drew lines then was going to get a worker to dig the ditch. The next week when I returned, I saw that right where I'd drawn those lines, a deep ditch had been dug. Some random people had seen it from afar and thought that I was looking for a treasure and, after I left, had gone to that spot looking for that treasure. So, I ended up not having to pay for that ditch. They wanted to get the treasure before we returned. Usually, you can find treasures in cemeteries.

In Shi'a Islam, there's the idea of the Hidden Imam. In this film we have the idea of hidden people.

You could interpret it like that, yes.

Does this have anything to do with the gravedigger scene in Hamlet*?*

I hadn't thought of that before. It could've existed in my subconscious, but not directly.

There's poetry throughout the movie. Who are the other poets?

Nobody knows; they're very ancient. I don't know their names. They're very popular but not famous.

Why is the idea of poetry important to the film?

Because I'd already had the idea for the screenplay. I've always read poetry, and once when I was reading this poem, "The Wind Will Carry Us," by Forough Farrokhzad, which I'd read many times before, I realized that it was very similar to my film. It's also the most Khayyam-like of Forough's poems. Then I decided to put it in the film. It's also an homage to Forough.

In this film, the film language is more poetic than ever before.

I think the same. No matter how much you may want to run away from it, you can't.

The main character is interesting in that he's not very sympathetic. You like this man, but you don't like what he does in some cases. Because he's not nice to the little boy. How did you find the actor, Behzad Dorani?*

---

* Bezhad Dorani worked as a television crewman prior to being cast in *The Wind Will Carry Us*. Kiarostami told various stories about how he met him.

He was the first one I found. For *Taste of Cherry*, I tested many people before I found Mr. Ershadi. But for this film, he was the first one. When I saw him, I realized this character could be many things: he could be likable, he could be a kind father, he could be a professional killer. So you can't quickly judge him. His face doesn't immediately give him away. And his face also has no nationality: not Iranian, not anything else. He belongs to everywhere. I thought this face could help with this ambiguity and this question of his identity. Since the film carries the question of who he is and what he is doing there until the sixtieth minute, you might expect him to kill the old lady. He has a cinematic face that can help move the film forward. When I saw the film last night, I realized he acted quite well.

There are characters like this one in your other films, like the director in And Life Goes On, *but this character seems different, in that his relationship to the people and the places he's going to is somewhat perverse. Would you agree with this?*

He's come here driven by the idea of death. He's really waiting for death, because his goal is dependent on someone else's death. Like the Quran-reading mullahs, who wait for someone's death [reference to people who get paid to read the Quran on people's graves]. Many people's lives are dependent on other people's death, like body-washers, gravediggers. They provide for their lives by waiting for others' death.

Is this self-criticism on your part, to have this character the way that he is?

To a degree, yes. Of course there's some of that character in me, just as the character of the kid is in me as well.

APPENDIX

The Iranian Who Won The World's Attention
by Godfrey Cheshire

When the 1997 Cannes Film Festival awarded the Palme d'Or, its highest honor, to Abbas Kiarostami's *Taste of Cherry* on its closing evening in May, the audience's acclamation had an extra edge of electricity. Two days before, the film's public debut had prompted standing ovations for the director before and after the screening. On awards night, as the applause returned, it indicated a signal event: the first time the Palme, Europe's equivalent of the Academy Award for Best Picture, had been bestowed on a film from Iran.

In part, the excitement that greeted the award reflected the dramatic way *Taste of Cherry* arrived in Cannes. Because the film concerns a man contemplating suicide, a taboo subject in the Islamic Republic, it has not been shown in Iran and was at first denied permission to leave that country, a decision that seemed ironclad before suddenly being reversed on the eve of the festival's opening, reportedly after appeals and discussions at the highest levels of the Iranian Government.

Yet the response to the film's victory at Cannes also seemed to indicate a widespread feeling, in the year the festival celebrated its 50th anniversary with a special award to Ingmar Bergman, that if the grand traditions of the art film are on the wane in much of the world, they remain very much alive in Mr. Kiarostami's Iran. Indeed, in 1997 few new films draw comparisons to classics like Mr. Bergman's *Wild Strawberries*, Michelangelo Antonioni's *Red Desert* or Jean-Luc Godard's *Contempt*. Mr. Kiarostami's movies not only evoke such parallels; they also seem to infuse the beleaguered art-film traditions with fresh urgency.

Back home in Tehran in August, the director had gained enough distance on the clamor of Cannes to recall it with amused detachment. Even at the time of his big victory, he says, he experienced it as if it were happening to someone else. "You gain it but don't feel it inside," he said with a smile. "You become a spectator, and you see that a man in glasses goes up from his seat to the stage, takes the Palme, says something in very bad French and then comes down again. That's all."

Something crucial is missing from that third-person recollection, however. In collecting his award, the bespectacled man exchanged a polite kiss with the beautiful French movie star presenting the award, Catherine Deneuve. In Iran, where men who win film prizes trade kisses only with other men, this brief offense to Islamic propriety ignited a firestorm of fundamentalist reaction that quickly eclipsed the news of Iran's triumph at Cannes.

While still in France, Mr. Kiarostami went on the rhetorical offensive, giving interviewers, even those who hadn't asked, his earnest version of "when in Rome…" It didn't work. On his return to Iran, a special welcoming reception at the airport was derailed by the threat of a protest by rightist militants. Mr. Kiarostami was whisked through customs and out a side door.

Such public dangers underscore the wisdom of the tradition of having Iranian homes face inward. The house in genteel northern Teheran that Mr. Kiarostami, who is 57 and divorced, has lived in for more than 20 years, and now shares with his 19-year-old son, Bahman, is no exception. Though it's situated at the end of a quiet alley off a quiet street, its outward face offers no more than the inscrutable gaze of a brick wall and a recessed doorway.

The Palme d'Or is now ensconced in the house, in a basement apartment that doubles as an office. It's surrounded by dozens of plaques, scrolls and statuettes; with more than 50 international prizes, Mr. Kiarostami is among the contemporary filmmakers with the most awards.

In addition to shelves of film books in several languages, the apartment's walls contain paintings and photographs. Some are by Mr. Kiarostami, who was a graphic artist and illustrator before turning to filmmaking. Other paintings are by, and were gifts from, the eminent Japanese director Akira Kurosawa, who has publicly championed the works of Mr. Kiarostami.

If the room's appointments project an air of international urbanity, so does Mr. Kiarostami's conversation. He makes reference at various points to Bertrand Russell and to John Richardson's biography of Picasso. He admits a liking for the American poets William Carlos Williams and Marianne Moore. In discussing his antipathy toward the sexual and violent fantasies of the Hollywood mainstream, he has favorable words for the independent filmmakers Jim Jarmusch and Jem Cohen.

MR. KIAROSTAMI'S OWN FILMMAKING began at the end of the 1960s when the loose-knit movement later labeled the Iranian New Wave was just gaining steam. Asked to start a filmmaking section for the Center for the Intellectual Development of Children and Young Adults (a Government organization that Iranians refer to as Kanoon), he began an institutional relationship that for the next 20 years let him develop his art while remaining sheltered from the pressures of commercial movie making.

One hallmark of Mr. Kiarostami's work is its esthetic consistency. "Bread and Alley," the first short he made, in 1970, has qualities that distinguish his films up to *Taste of Cherry*: a lyrical but concrete feel for the particulars of place and visual atmosphere; a way of eliciting strikingly natural performances from nonactors; and stories in which an anecdotal surface disguises a rich substratum of philosophical, allegorical or social concerns.

The deep, searching humanism that forms the ethical heart of his work, and that has evoked comparisons to Italian neo-realist masterpieces like Vittorio De Sica's *Bicycle Thieves*, was noted in the series of shorts that he made for Kanoon, and in his two features of the 1970s, *The Traveler*, about a boy who goes to desperate lengths to reach a football match, and *The Report*, a harrowing account of a failing marriage.

Mr. Kiarostami did not consider leaving the country during the Iranian revolution of 1978-79, he said, "because of a revolution going on in my own house." His own marriage was failing.

Once the Islamic Republic decided that a productive, culturally responsible film industry offered more benefits than the revolutionary practice of torching cinemas, Mr. Kiarostami was persuaded to make another feature. *Where Is the Friend's House?* (1987), a simple tale of a rural boy trying to return a friend's notebook after school, won Mr. Kiarostami instant fame at Western film festivals. It also nudged him into the de facto trilogy that would secure his reputation.

Just after a 1990 earthquake devastated the area where he shot *Where Is the Friend's House?*, Mr. Kiarostami went back to the region, to ascertain whether his young actors had survived. A year later he turned this experience into the meditative, documentary-like fiction of *And Life Goes On*, in which filmmaking itself becomes part of the humanistic inquiry. That was followed in 1994 by *Through the Olive Trees*, in which the shooting of the previous film was recreated as the backdrop to a tale about the unrequited love of two bit players, both victims of the earthquake's tragedy.

Mr. Kiarostami's films don't so much avoid political concerns as subsume them in broader investigations, often concerning the ways obsession, compassion and art intertwine. *Close-Up* (1990), the most famous of his several documentaries, depicts the trial of a poor man who gained illicit entree into the upper classes by posing as a famous film director.

Taste of Cherry is at once consistent with his previous work and a risky departure. Treating the proscribed subject of suicide, it follows a prosperous-seeming, fiftyish man named Badii (played by Homayoun Ershadi) as he drives around Teheran trying to find someone who will help him kill himself. His passengers include a young soldier, a seminarian and an elderly taxidermist, who advance different arguments against his deadly wish.

ASKED IF THE STORY REFLECTED his own grappling with suicide, Mr. Kiarostami said simply, "Yes, but that is private." He added that when he was young and watched his father endure an agonizing illness, he thought about the right to end one's life and decided that religion did not offer the "higher wisdom" on the issue.

Is such wisdom the ultimate subject of *Taste of Cherry*? Mr. Kiarostami gives the more persuasive arguments against suicide to the taxidermist—a kind of natural philosopher—rather than to the seminarian, evoking disagreements over the relative uses of philosophy and religion that occupied Islamic thought during its medieval golden age. The same question, obviously, can be applied to whole societies. Mr. Kiarostami listened to this reasoning, then replied with a firm nod.

Pierre Rissient, an executive with Ciby 2000, the French company that handles worldwide sales of *Taste of Cherry*, says that Mr. Kiarostami "proceeds the way the Greek philosophers like Heraclitus do, or Chinese figures like Laotzu, or Japanese Zen poets like Basho—the poetry is completely linked with philosophy."

In *Taste of Cherry* it's also linked with Mr. Kiarostami's painterly way with landscapes and light, and with one unusual technique that few viewers would probably detect. None of the actors in the film ever met one another, the director explained. When Badii talked with his various passengers, and they with him, the person in the opposite seat was always in reality Mr. Kiarostami. He would film one side of a conversation, then change actors and film the other side. Considering the subject under discussion, this lends the film an air of uncanny intimacy.

While such inventiveness might seem to have a natural place in American art houses, the United States has only recently begun to open up to films from Iran. When *Taste of Cherry* was chosen to appear in the New York festival, it did not have an American distributor (as it turned out, Zeitgeist Films picked it up last Monday, and plans to release it early next year). But that was all the more reason for it to be at Lincoln Center, said Richard Peña, chairman of the festival's selection committee.

Watching Mr. Kiarostami's film, said Mr. Peña, "you sense that you're in the presence of someone who's airing issues of extreme importance."

"These are real issues that all of us in our own way face in our own lives," he said, "and so rarely are they treated on film: the sense of crying out to others, of needing others, of trying to create a bridge to others. So few works are able to express that with any percentage of the power that I think this film reaches so simply."

First published in the *New York Times*
September 28, 1997

Thanks

From the time these interviews were conducted, I've benefited from help from various people in having them translated and moved toward publication. These include, but are not limited to: Jamsheed Akrami, Mohammad Atebbai, Parto Mohtadi, Naghmeh Sohrabi, Olga Davidson and The Ilex Foundation, and Dorna Khazeni.

Thanks also to mk2, Janus Films/The Criterion Collection, Celluloid Dreams, Ahmad Kiarostami and the Kiarostami Foundation for their support and help in pulling this book together.

In the preparation of this manuscript, I was fortunate to have the expert translation skills of Tania Ahmadi, who was able to make sense of a heteroclite mass of old audiotapes and texts.

And I owe endless thanks to editor Jim Colvill, whose extraordinarily scrupulous, intelligent, thorough-going work brought this series of interviews to its final form.

About the author

Godfrey Cheshire is a New York-based filmmaker and critic whose writings on Iranian cinema have appeared in publications including the *New York Times*, *Variety*, *Film Comment*, *Sight & Sound*, *Cineaste*, *The Village Voice* and *Dissent*.